Shakespeare
Man of the Theatre

Wendy Greenhill

Head of Education
Royal Shakespeare Company

Paul Wignall

Heinemann
LIBRARY

First published in Great Britain by Heinemann Library,
Halley Court, Jordan Hill, Oxford OX2 8EJ,
a division of Reed Educational and Professional Publishing Ltd.
Heinemann is a registered trademark of Reed Educational &
Professional Publishing Limited.

OXFORD MELBOURNE AUCKLAND
JOHANNESBURG BLANTYRE GABORONE
IBADAN PORTSMOUTH NH (USA) CHICAGO

Typeset by Wyvern 21 Ltd, Bristol
Illustrations by Jeff Edwards
Printed in Hong Kong by Wing King Tong

03 02 01 00 99
10 9 8 7 6 5 4 3 2 1

ISBN 0 431 07514 X

British Library Cataloguing in Publication Data
Greenhill, Wendy
    Shakespeare, man of the theatre
    1. Shakespeare, William, 1564–1616 – Biography –Juvenile
    literature   2. Theater – England – History – 16th century –
    Juvenile literature   3. Great Britain – Social life and
    customs – 16th century – Juvenile literature
    I. Title   II. Wignall, Paul
    822.3'3

Acknowledgements
The Publishers would like to thank the following for permission to
reproduce photographs:
Bibliothek der Reichsuniversitet, Utrecht, pp. 71, 108; Edinburgh
University Library, p. 5; Mary Evans Picture Library, p. 44; The Public
Records Office, London, p. 174; Shakespeare Birthplace Trust, Stratford,
pp. 1, 21, 155; by permission of The Trustees of Dulwich Picture Gallery,
pp. 55, 112.

Cover photograph: Portrait of Shakespeare, from the title page of First
Folio, published in 1623, reproduced by permission of The Shakespeare
Birthplace Trust, Stratford-upon-Avon.

Our thanks to Brian Tyler for his comments in the preparation of this
book.

For more information about Heinemann Library books, or to order,
please phone 01865 888066, or send a fax to 01865 314091. You can
visit our web site at *www.heinemann.co.uk*

Contents

Note on the Glossary

Terms listed in the Glossary are indicated by a † symbol at their first mention in each chapter.

1

INTRODUCTION: A PROCESSION IN LONDON, 1604

At eleven o'clock on the morning of 15 March 1604, an enormous procession began to wind its way from the Tower of London. Everyone there counted themselves part of the royal court, including the entire Government of England – bishops, knights and judges, barons, earls and viscounts. At Barking churchyard they were greeted by songs from the children of Christ's Hospital school. They marched along Fenchurch Street, Gracechurch Street and into Cheapside where the great conduit which supplied the citizens with clean water was running with claret wine, then down past St Paul's Cathedral and along Fleet Street until at Temple Bar they left the City of London and entered Westminster. Up the Strand they walked, past the fine houses of the most powerful noblemen of the kingdom, to Charing Cross and on to Westminster Abbey until, turning left, they entered the Palace of Whitehall.

In the centre of the procession rode King James I of England. He had been proclaimed king almost exactly 12 months earlier after the death of Queen Elizabeth I. Travelling south from Scotland where he was already king, James had not gone immediately to Westminster before for fear of the plague† which was raging there. His coronation in Westminster Abbey on 25 July 1603 went ahead with little ceremony, again because of the plague. Today was the first official opportunity for the large crowds who lined the route in London to see their new king.

King James I in the Royal Procession, 15 March 1604. An illustration from Michael van Meer's *Album Amicorum*.

The procession from the Tower to Whitehall was a show of strength. The spectacle, and the official speeches and poems read along the way, displayed the magnificence of the king and therefore the power of England. The foreign ambassadors among the cheering crowds were expected to be impressed by what they saw, and to report to their own kings that England was not a country to be trifled with.

But behind the show of strength and unity all was not well. The London through which James rode that March afternoon in 1604 was like a miniature of the condition of England. In its narrow streets and lanes there was grinding poverty, there were merchants made rich by trade, and there was the nobility, traditional authority desperate to maintain status by a show of magnificence, financed by a debt-ridden king.

When James became its king, England was undergoing painful social and economic changes. It is estimated that in the previous 50 years the population had shot up from about three million to about four million. The growth in the number of mouths to feed was not matched by increased food production. This led in turn to a rise in prices and a drop in wages. Families began to move around the country looking for work. The subsistence economy of the medieval countryside, where families and villages produced enough for their own needs, was replaced by a market economy in which larger landowners supplied (at a price) the food and bought up the farms of those struggling to survive. The rural England through which James travelled from Scotland in 1603 was a place of poverty, starvation and discontent, which from time to time erupted into open rebellion against the wealthier families.

These families – the gentry[†] – were the new force in the land. As they gained more economic power, so they expected to exercise greater political power. In the later years of the reign of Queen Elizabeth I, the House of Commons, which was made up of the land-owning gentry and influential merchants, began to demand that its voice be heard. The traditional authority of the monarch and the great noblemen dating back to the Middle Ages was challenged by a more modern attitude. The gentry and the merchants, as the suppliers and organizers of the wealth of the nation, wanted to have their hands on the reins of power and to control the overspending of the royal court.

There were other pressures on James. The bishops of the Church of England walking ahead of him in the procession were reminders of two other controversies already being played out. King Henry VIII's separation of the Church in England from the authority of the Pope in Rome in 1534 had plunged the country into religious discontent. For the next 30 years there were open power struggles between Catholics[†] and Protestants[†]. Elizabeth had tried to paper the cracks but in reality she was ruling a people divided by their religion. When it could be believed, or imagined, that Catholics were plotting to overthrow the monarch in favour of a candidate who would restore Catholicism, then religious belief became a test of loyalty as well. To be a Catholic was to be suspected of treason.

If some of the citizens of London who greeted James with outward shows of loyalty were in fact secret Catholics, many others were openly Puritan. Puritanism[†] had developed during the 16th century as

7

a form of Christianity whose followers believed that people should have a direct relationship with God, expressed in a simple moral way of life that would 'purify' society. Puritans were men and women trying to lead a good and honest life. They believed in hard work, and disliked any outward show in religion and extravagance in public or private life. Throughout James's reign they were bitter opponents of his over-spending and what they saw as the immorality of his court. The Puritans and their sympathizers among the gentry and merchant class came increasingly to hold the country's purse-strings, much to James's irritation. After his death in 1625 their opposition to the new king, Charles I, gradually intensified until it erupted into a civil war in which the Puritan tendency was victorious. Charles was executed in 1649 and replaced as head of state by Oliver Cromwell, who had been a leader of the king's parliamentary opponents.

The London through which James rode in March 1604, no less than the England across which he had travelled a year earlier, was a place of contradiction. The old order – the authority of the nobility, the absolute rule of the king – was under threat from a new and increasingly powerful political and religious alliance of landowners and merchants.

Beneath the paper-thin crust of unity which the royal procession was intended both to establish and re-inforce, was a seething mass of discontent, fed by poverty, overcrowding and starvation as well as by religious disagreements and traitorous plotting. No wonder that concealed beneath the fine silks of the clothes he wore, James had on – as he always did – a quilted jacket, padded to protect him from an assassin's knife.

THE KING'S MEN

Somewhere near the front of the procession, among the grooms and gentlemen of the royal household, there was a group of nine men, wearing crimson cloaks made from material specially provided for the occasion. They were the king's own company of actors, the King's Men, who had received the royal authority on 19 May 1603:

> 'Know ye that we... have licensed and authorised... these our servants Lawrence Fletcher, William Shakespeare, Richard Burbage, Augustine Phillips, John Heminges, Henry Condell, William Sly, Robert Armin, Richard Cowley and the rest of their associates freely to use and exercise the art and faculty of playing comedies, tragedies, histories, interludes, morals, pastorals, stage-plays and such others like... as well for the recreation of our loving subjects, as for our solace and pleasure when we shall think good to see them... '

This document tells us a great deal about the status and conditions of actors (or 'players' as they were known, and we will use this term from now on) at the beginning of the 17th century:

1. The King's Men were licensed. Like all players they were controlled by the state and protected by powerful noblemen, and the plays they performed were censored by a state official, the Master of the Revels†, on behalf of the Lord Chamberlain†.

2. Companies of players were part of the household of their patrons† but they were also independent. The nine men named in James's letter were sharers† in the company, entitled to a part of the proceeds from the performances they gave. They might employ other players, or train young players, but the risks and the

9

profits were theirs. They were businessmen as well as players or writers.

3. From our modern point of view, the theatrical life in the London of Elizabeth I and James I is overwhelmingly dominated by one name: William Shakespeare. It is vital to remember, though, that this is not how it would have appeared to his contemporaries. He was one among many. He was one of nine sharers in the King's Men. He wrote plays for them (about two each year) but so did many other writers. He acted in those plays – at least in the early years of their time together – and many of the sharers in the King's Men had been colleagues in one company or another for more than ten years before the king gave them his name. Shakespeare became wealthy not least because of his shares in the company – but so did all the others. However, Shakespeare seems to us today to be a special case. His plays are still performed, moving us to tears or making us laugh, when those of many of his contemporaries are gathering dust on library shelves. But we cannot understand him properly if we don't also understand that in his day he was a professional actor, a businessman and a courtier, whose work reflects the world around him.

4. Players were expected to have a wide range of plays to perform, and the demands of playgoers were insatiable – from the king right down to the groundlings who paid a few pence to stand and watch the plays. New plays, in many styles, rolled off the production line much faster than films today emerge from Hollywood. A playwright might produce three, four or more plays a year, alone or collaborating with others, and companies were in open competition to come up

with a hit. They were in the business of pleasing audiences.

5. Players had a number of audiences. There were the public playhouses in London – The Globe, The Fortune, The Rose, and others. There were the regular tours around the country, especially when the plague closed the London theatres. There were performances for their own patrons, in the great country houses or in London. And there were the performances at court commanded by the king himself, either as part of the annual festivities at Christmas, for example, or to contribute to the entertainment laid on for foreign ambassadors and princes. The King's Men in particular were not only in the business of pleasing their audience, they also had to please the king.

Of course pleasing can involve challenging. As we will see, the playhouses (as theatres were called) shared the same stresses and strains as the rest of society. The plays not only offered their audiences a comforting glimpse of national unity and authority but also lifted the lid on discontentments within society and showed the witches' cauldron of fears that were bubbling just beneath the surface. Not for nothing were playhouses seen as dangerous places.

A MIRROR UP TO NATURE

What, then, was the place of the theatre in the England of Elizabeth and James, and of William Shakespeare? First of all, it was on the edges of society, both in fact and in people's imagination. The first playhouses were built in the Liberties†, north of the city and on the south bank of the River Thames, so called because they were places outside the bounds of the city's authority. This independence was reinforced, first by the support of noble patrons, including the king, and then by their popularity with playgoers. But plays and playhouses were marginal in a second sense. When Hamlet reminds the players that

> '...the purpose of playing... was and is to hold as 'twere the mirror up to nature, to show virtue her own feature, scorn her own image, and the very age and body of the time his form and pressure...'
>
> *Hamlet*, Act 3 Scene 2, lines 22–24

he is saying that in playhouses playgoers see themselves reflected not as they would like to be but as they are. The stage of the playhouse and the words the players speak capture the anxieties and fears, the joys and hopes of the world outside.

The society in which Shakespeare lived and worked was trapped between old ideas of authority and the demands of rapid social change, between a king trying to embody unity through magnificent displays of power, and seething discontent just beneath the surface. Put in another way, Shakespeare's England could not avoid the gap between words and deeds. The wise person listened with a good dose of suspicion. In London and the Palace of Whitehall (the centre of the king's court and government), survival meant knowing who you trusted, and knowing that you could trust almost nobody.

Once again, the playhouses were the perfect place to reflect this war between trust and suspicion. Plays frequently reveal that gap between what we say we will do and what we actually do. That is to say, they depend upon dramatic irony†: the moments when an audience is aware of something of which a character in the play is ignorant, be it a banana skin, a hidden dagger, or a promise that is about to be broken.

Theatre stands on the margins of society. When it is given enough freedom it can show us as we are, not as we think we are. And it does so by revealing the gap between what we say we will do and what we may actually do. But theatre also shows us how we can be, when we are at our best, and what happens when the gap between words and deeds has been closed; what happens when we learn to trust. As we shall see, in Shakespeare's working life he moved constantly between the language of suspicion and the language of trust. Judging by the kind of plays he was writing at this time, as Shakespeare walked towards the Palace of Whitehall in the late afternoon of 15 March 1604, he was perhaps at his most suspicious and cynical.

FOUR PLAYS

Four plays from these years are shot through with a vein of cynicism and raise uncomfortable moral questions about love, sex, politics and war. In *Measure for Measure* and *Macbeth*, Shakespeare explores problems of kingship; in *Troilus and Cressida* and *Timon of Athens*, he shows the destructive descent from sexual love (*Troilus*) and wealth (*Timon*) into suspicion and cynicism.

Lack of trust is a keynote throughout these plays. People eavesdrop and spy on one another, trick and deceive, conceal and evade. Sex is traded for hard currency, for favours, for survival. Ideals dissolve in the tough world of lust, politics and war. These plays all question the nature of love and the possibility of fidelity, and take a sceptical view of politics and morals. Everything and everyone has their price.

TROILUS AND CRESSIDA

The action of *Troilus and Cressida* takes place during the war between Ancient Greece and Troy, the subject of one of the oldest, and greatest, works of Western literature: *The Iliad*. Parts of this epic poem, written nearly 3000 years earlier by Homer, had been translated by George Chapman in 1598 and immediately became a best seller. It is the story of a war fought over a woman, Helen, the most beautiful woman in the world and the wife of a Greek king. Helen has been abducted and taken to Troy by one of the Trojan king's sons. The Greeks follow and besiege the city to get her back. Shakespeare's play takes place in the middle of the siege and concerns a love-affair between the Trojan, Troilus, and the Greek, Cressida. Their love is encouraged by Cressida's uncle, Pandarus, but broken by wider political considerations. Pandarus's cynicism twists the love of Troilus and Cressida into a nasty sexual grope, just as the vicious satire of the Greek soldier Thersites changes the bravery of the warriors into a tawdry fight between men for a woman who is not worth it. Even the final battle between the two great heroes, Achilles the Greek and Hector the Trojan, degenerates into mere brutality. Hector is surrounded by Achilles and his men, the Myrmidons:

Hector: I am unarmed. Forgo this vantage, Greek.
Achilles: Strike, fellows, strike. This is the man I seek
[The Myrmidons kill Hector]
So, Ilium, fall thou. Now, Troy, sink down.
On Myrmidons, and cry you all amain,
'Achilles hath the mighty Hector slain!'
Troilus and Cressida, Act 5 Scene 9, lines 9–14

Thersites' language is shot through with images of disease, turning Troy into a plague-ridden city, and giving love the colours of death:

Thersites: Now the rotten diseases of the south, guts-
griping, ruptures, catarrhs, loads o' gravel
i' th' back, lethargies, cold palsies, and the
like, take and take again such preposterous
discoveries.
Troilus and Cressida, Act 5 Scene 1, lines 17–21

Troilus and Cressida is an astonishing play, remorse-lessly burying human values under lust and lying, death and disease.

MEASURE FOR MEASURE

Shakespeare makes the city of Vienna, in which *Measure for Measure* is sct, as full of infection as Troy. Perhaps disease was on his mind, as the London theatres had been closed from May 1603 to April 1604 because of plague, and it is likely that the play was written some months after they re-opened. It was certainly played before James on 26 December 1604.

The play concerns Isabella, a young woman about to enter a nunnery, whose brother Claudio has been harshly condemned to death for immorality. The Duke of Vienna has gone away, leaving the vice-ridden city in the control of his deputy, Angelo, a man noted for his strict morals. Angelo is determined to clean things up. Isabella pleads for Claudio's life and Angelo, overcome with lust for her, agrees to spare Claudio if she will sleep with him. She appears to agree but Angelo is tricked when another woman (Mariana, whom Angelo has abandoned) comes to him instead. The Duke returns, punishes Angelo for his hypocrisy, forces him to marry Mariana, and marries Isabella himself.

Deeply serious as well as full of knockabout humour, set in brothels and prisons, the play explores sex and death and the abuse of power, while allowing the wise ruler to see the truth and judge well. It also shows clearly the theatrical nature of kingship at this time. The Duke creates a dramatic scene by which to make known his judgements – much as King James liked to rule by dramatic effects. But if the play seems to offer King James a mirror for his own view of justice, it has many painful undercurrents. Every character is ambiguous – of none can it be said, she is wholly good, he utterly bad. Perhaps Shakespeare wants to show that justice is not a simple matter – it has to take account of the fact that we are all 'desperately human' (*Measure for Measure*, Act 4 Scene 2, line 147).

TIMON OF ATHENS

Modern scholarship has shown that *Timon of Athens* is almost certainly a collaboration between Shakespeare and a playwright nearly 20 years his junior, Thomas Middleton. Middleton may well have had a hand in *Measure for Measure* and *Macbeth* as well, so we may assume he worked closely with the King's Men from about 1602. *Timon* may even be a revision of an original play by Middleton. Probably written in 1604, the play as we have it (there is no record of its performance at this time) is not unlike earlier, medieval plays which showed the journey of a good man through the temptations of life. But *Timon* is a grim story. It shows a rich and generous man's fall into poverty. As he does so his friends abandon him. In the second part he becomes rich again but he is now bitter and leaves Athens in disgust:

> 'Nothing I'll bear from thee
> But nakedness, thou detestable town...
> The gods confound – hear me you good gods all –
> Th' Athenians, both within and out that wall;
> And grant, as Timon grows, his hate may grow
> To the whole race of mankind, high and low.
> Amen.'
>
> *Timon of Athens*, Act 4 Scene 1, lines 32–40

Timon's bitterness drives him away from civilization, from other people and out into the desert where, at last, he prepares for death by digging his own grave and writing his epitaph. The pursuit of wealth which was the basis of his former generosity and the cause of his fall, is now the focus of his contempt:

> 'What a god's gold,
> That he is worshipped in a baser temple
> Than where swine feed!
> To thee be worship, and thy saints for aye
> Be crowned with plagues, that thee alone obey.'
>
> *Timon of Athens*, Act 5 Scene 1, lines 46–52

For Christianity the desert is traditionally the place where God is found; the wilderness the place of truth. But at the end of his journey Timon has no room for joy or comfort. His epitaph is a curse:

> 'Seek not my name. A plague consume
>   You wicked caitiffs left!
> Here lie I, Timon, who alive
>   All living men did hate.'

Timon of Athens, Act 5 Scene 5, lines 73–76

MACBETH

The previous three plays that we have begun to explore, from Shakespeare's middle years, are comparatively little known and two at least are unfortunately rarely performed. The fourth, *Macbeth*, is one of his most famous.

Probably written in 1606, *Macbeth* explores problems that terrified King James. The king lived in fear of assassination and of witchcraft. In *Macbeth*, a Scottish nobleman is encouraged by three 'weird' sisters (witches) to kill King Duncan and take the throne himself. 'Weird' is an old English word for fate or destiny, and the women are 'weird' because they foretell the future. Macbeth and his wife come to embody evil, and the portrayal of their collapse under the weight of guilty consciences and their destruction by the forces of good, would have pleased James. But, as always with Shakespeare, what seems to be simply a story of good overcoming evil is, in reality much more complex.

Macbeth explores what it means to make choices. Should Macbeth and his wife be loyal to their king, or do they take advantage of an opportunity to seize power? But the human capacity to choose is undercut by fate. The weird sisters' promise to Macbeth – that he will be 'king hereafter' – seems to remove his duty to act morally. But this is a delusion. As the play unfolds we, with the Macbeths, become painfully aware that destiny and choice are two edges of the same sword.

As the play proceeds down its dark and murderous path we are constantly invited to consider how far the Macbeths are responsible for what they do. Lady Macbeth seems to be the stronger of the two at first, but she is finally broken by the guilt she cannot easily acknowledge. Macbeth's conscience never lets him forget the difference between what he should have done and what he did do. He should not have killed Duncan; he should have chosen differently.

As the Macbeths embark on their career of murder, a gap begins to open up between the way they must behave in public and their private world of guilt and fear. They are mistaken if they think they can leave their consciences behind. But as public figures, exercising power, actors on the political stage, they must do so. *Macbeth* gives little ground for hope that kings can sleep easy in their beds – their role is intolerable, they cannot wash the blood from their hands. In the end Lady Macbeth dies, unable to deal with the pressure of guilt. As he hears of her death, Macbeth accepts the futility of what he has done.

'Life's but a walking shadow, a poor player
That struts and frets his hour upon the stage,
And then is heard no more. It is a tale
Told by an idiot, full of sound and fury,
Signifying nothing.'

Macbeth, Act 5 Scene 5, lines 23–27

2
STRATFORD-UPON-AVON

We don't know the precise date of William Shakespeare's birth. His name appears in the register of baptisms of Holy Trinity Church in Stratford-upon-Avon on 26 April 1564. Children were usually baptized within two or three days of their birth, and tradition has put Shakespeare's birthday as 23 April: St George's Day. It is a nice idea to link the birthday of our greatest playwright with the festival of England's patron saint, but we have no way of knowing the actual date of his birth, and it is unlikely we ever will.

What sort of place was Stratford in 1564? Like most English market towns, Stratford owed its growth first to the fact that some 368 years earlier (in 1196) it had been granted the status of a borough†. This gave the people who lived there (the burgesses†) certain rights and privileges. As freemen, burgesses controlled their towns independently of the great landowners. They were not tied to the land, but bought local farmers' products and sold them both locally and further afield. They might also manufacture goods from some of the locally produced raw materials, again selling them both locally and more widely across England.

Such towns were usually situated at strategic communication points. Stratford's bridge over the River Avon was built in about 1490 with money provided by Sir Hugh Clopton (who also built New Place, Shakespeare's Stratford home from 1597 until his death in 1616). The bridge, which remains one of the main routes through Stratford, gave a boost to the town's trading connections between the Midlands and London.

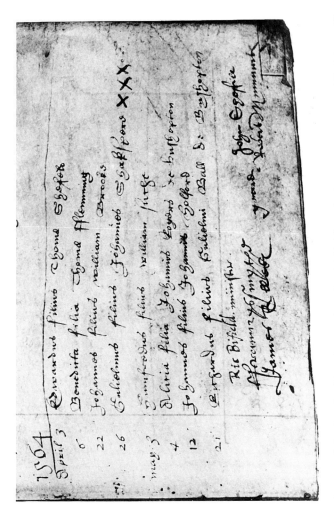

A page of the Stratford baptism register for 1564. Near the bottom you can see 'Gulielmus filius Johannes Shakspear' (William, son of John Shakespeare). The register is now in The Shakespeare Birthplace Trust, Stratford-upon-Avon.

By the time the Clopton Bridge was built, Stratford's life was largely controlled by the Guild[†] of the Holy Cross, an association of town tradesmen, merchants, and local landowning gentry[†]. The Guild managed the town's prosperity to the advantage of those who were creating it but it also provided for the public good. By 1547, repairs to the bridge, building and maintaining almshouses (special accommodation for the poor and elderly) and the funding of the town's grammar school[†], were all the responsibility of the Guild.

In that year, 17 years before William Shakespeare was born, great social changes came to Stratford. These were triggered partly by the religious upheaval of the Reformation[†] and partly by the new economic conditions in England. The Guild of the Holy Cross, along with many other religious foundations, was abolished and its property confiscated by the king. The town was left in a state of chaos until 1553 when the new king, Edward VI, granted a charter for a new arrangement in Stratford. The Guild's duties were taken over by a bailiff[†] and fourteen aldermen[†], prominent local men who were responsible for the bridge, the almshouses and the school, and for paying the vicar. The property confiscated from the Guild was restored to help the new Corporation[†] to carry out their duties. They were also allowed to appoint 14 burgesses, other townsmen, who all had particular duties. Two, for example, were required to keep account of the town's finances and property. In 1564 these responsible posts were held by John Taylor and John Shakespeare.

JOHN SHAKESPEARE AND MARY ARDEN

If we are going to understand William Shakespeare, the playwright who was also a landowner, a trader, a father and husband, and sharer[†] in perhaps the most important theatre company of his day, then we have to understand something of his background – the expectations and ambitions of the family into which he was born as well as the society in which he grew up.

John and Mary Shakespeare, William's parents, were typical of those who created, prospered under and sometimes became the victims of, the great changes of the 16th century. Their story will not help us understand their son's exceptional gifts as a poet and playwright, but it may help us understand how he used those gifts to make his way in the world.

William's grandfather, Richard Shakespeare, was a tenant farmer at Snitterfield, a village four miles north of Stratford. His landlord was Richard Arden of Wilmcote, a village to the west of Stratford and about three miles away. By the 1540s, Richard Shakespeare was fairly prosperous and by the time of his death in 1560 he had become an influential and wealthy man in the village. His story shows how it was possible for tenant farmers to climb the social and economic ladder during the boom years in the middle of the 16th century.

Richard Shakespeare's son John moved to Stratford as a young man. He became a glover and whittawer – a worker in white leather, the luxury end of the market.

Leather-making and -working was one of the most important trades in the Midlands in the 16th century, and some of the wealthiest citizens of Stratford were associated with it. John was probably apprenticed[†] to Thomas Dickson, who had family connections with Snitterfield. Whatever the precise and personal reasons for his move, it was typical of the period that the son of a successful tenant farmer would become an apprentice in a trade where he could learn a skill and take the family another step up the ladder.

Leather-making is a good example of the shape of the new prosperity. Glovers bought animal skins, prepared them by the process of tanning, then turned them into a range of goods, not only gloves, but also belts and bags, for instance. Like most trades it required capital – money to buy the skins and to meet the costs of preparation had to be found in advance of the income from selling the finished product. And like most trades it was carried out at or near the tradesman's home. When, before 1552, John Shakespeare set up in Henley Street in Stratford, it was accepted that he would live 'over the shop', although some of the smellier parts of the business (the tanning which used raw materials such as urine and alum on the skins) were probably carried out elsewhere in Stratford.

By 1557 John Shakespeare was ready to marry. Once more family connections were called in. Mary Arden was 17, a daughter of the late Richard Arden of Wilmcote who had been Richard Shakespeare's landlord. We do not know where the Ardens lived in Wilmcote. The place now visited by tourists as Mary Arden's House never had any connection with the family, though it is typical of the sort of place they would have lived in.

Mary Arden must have been a capable young woman. When her father died in December 1556 she took charge of the property arrangements. She also inherited some of her father's land. John Shakespeare may have fallen in love with her but he also made a sound practical choice. She was wealthy, and her income, which legally passed to John, would have enabled him to keep his growing business on a sound footing. She could also run a household, and was experienced in managing property and money. Mary would become not only John's wife, but also effectively his business partner.

This too was typical of the time. The relationship between men and women in marriage was changing in the 16th century. Traditionally, legally, and very often actually, a man, as husband and father, expected obedience from his wife and children. But reformed Christianity in the 16th century was beginning to stress the importance of companionship in marriage. Husband and wife were still a long way from being equals, but women had important roles to play, sharing in the responsibilities and duties of households. Of course there were those who thought the changes were upsetting a fundamental, God-given order: the woman's place was simply to be obedient to her husband. But in fact it was impossible to run any complex household, either of merchants, tradesmen, or farmers, without husbands and wives sharing day-to-day decision-making. The gap between the public assertion of patriarchy (rule by men) and the reality of marriages as practical partnerships led to a good deal of anxiety, expressed both in jokes and cautionary stories about dominant women. The proper relationship between men and women in love and preparation for marriage was to become one of the most important themes in many of Shakespeare's plays.

THE RISE OF JOHN SHAKESPEARE

As a rising young glover, John Shakespeare needed to play a part in Stratford's public life. In 1556 he was an official beer-taster, two years later he was a constable, keeping the peace, and the next year an affeeror – which meant he assessed the fines that citizens had to pay. In 1561 he became one of the 14 burgesses or town councillors, rising to become chamberlain†, in charge of the town's finances, in 1564, the year of William's birth. John was obviously liked and trusted. In 1565 he was elected one of the 14 aldermen, the senior officials who ran Stratford. Three years later, on 1 October 1568, he took up the post of bailiff for the year, the key post in the town's life. In the 16 years since his first mention in the Stratford records – when he was fined in 1552 for keeping a dunghill in Henley Street – John had risen to a position of trust in his adopted home town.

THE SHAKESPEARE FAMILY

William was the third child, and eldest son, of the eight sons and daughters of John and Mary Shakespeare. Their first child, Joan, was born in 1558 and died as an infant. In 1562 another daughter, Margaret, was born but she died a year later. William came next, in April 1564. Within months the plague† was raging, killing old and young alike (see Chapter 6 – nearly 20 per cent of the population of Stratford died of plague in the second half of 1564). John and Mary's anxiety that their first son would follow his sisters to an early grave can easily be imagined.

The next child, Gilbert, was born in October 1566. He never married. William's story might well have been Gilbert's, but for his talent as a player and writer. Gilbert was a successful businessman with interests in London and Stratford. He died in February 1612.

Joan Shakespeare (it was common for children to be given the names of dead brothers or sisters) was born in April 1569. She married, became Joan Hart, remained in Stratford, had three sons, and died in 1646, aged 76.

John and Mary's next child, Anne, was born in September 1571 and died at the age of seven in April 1579. We know almost nothing about their son Richard, except that he was born in March 1574 and died in Stratford in February 1613.

The eighth and last child, Edmund, was baptized on 3 May 1580. Eventually he followed William to London where he became a player but died in December 1607, still only 27. He was buried in the church of St Mary Overy, near The Globe theatre, on the south bank of the Thames, which was frozen over by a great frost. Edmund had made no name for himself as an actor but the funeral was an expensive one. Presumably it was paid for by his older brother, William.

The children of John and Mary Shakespeare are to all intents and purposes a typical prosperous small-town family of their time. Some died young but one lived to be 76. Those who grew to be adults kept more or less strong links with their home town but, as might be expected, the sons also had links with London, the centre of English life and trade. They differ little from the families of many other successful merchants and tradesmen living in the market towns of England in the 16th century. Only the remarkable career of one son lifts them out of obscurity.

SHAKESPEARE AT SCHOOL

John and Mary Shakespeare were quite possibly unable to read or write. Their business as glovers, and John's involvement with town affairs, were conducted by word of mouth. This was not unusual. If the need arose – for legal documents, for instance – then the services of a lawyer or a clerk could always be obtained. But the newly prosperous merchant and tradesmen families valued education – for their sons. All over England grammar schools were established, many of them replacing church or cathedral schools. In Stratford in 1553, as we have seen, responsibility for the school passed from the old Guild to the new town Corporation. One of the advantages of being a burgess was that your children could be educated there free of charge. We have no proof, but it is almost certain that John Shakespeare would have made use of this privilege. Sometime in 1570, when he was six, William Shakespeare probably began a course of education lasting for some eight or nine years.

The bailiff and aldermen of Stratford paid their schoolmaster well and so attracted good teachers. If Shakespeare was at the school when he was six (in 1570) the master was Walter Roche, though the youngest pupils were normally taught by an assistant. When Roche left in 1571 he was replaced by Simon Hunt, who remained for four years. Between 1575 and 1579 the master was Thomas Jenkins, an Oxford graduate who had spent the previous nine years as a teacher in Warwick. When Jenkins moved on he arranged that his successor should be John Cottom, another Oxford man. Cottom remained until 1581, when he went home to Lancashire.

It is possible that Simon Hunt had Catholic[†] leanings – a man of that name arrived at the Catholic university at Douai (in modern Belgium) in 1575 and became a Jesuit[†] in Rome in 1578. It is certain that John Cottom was a Catholic. His brother Thomas was a Jesuit and so seen as a spy. He was arrested in England in 1580, carrying a letter addressed to a man in Shottery – a village just outside Stratford. Thomas was tried in November 1581 and executed in May 1582. Perhaps John Cottom returned to Lancashire to avoid any fallout from his brother's trial and death. As we shall see, these connections have given weight to speculations about what William Shakespeare did after he left school.

When John Shakespeare moved from his father's home in Snitterfield to become a glover in Stratford, his opinions, knowledge and attitudes would have differed little from those he left behind. When William Shakespeare walked the few hundred yards through Stratford from his home in Henley Street to the grammar school in the Guild Hall he was entering another world.

To have a grammar school education was not only to learn the skills of reading and writing, it also opened up a world of learning, and attitudes to life, that separated schoolboys forever from their parents. School days were long – mornings from 6 or 7 to 11, and in the afternoons from 1 to 5 – and had two main ele-

29

ments. First the boys learned Latin grammar and then used it both to learn a collection of useful words, phrases and simple ideas, and to put these to use in writing increasingly complicated Latin sentences. From the age of nine they would also be reading and translating political speeches by the Ancient Roman author Cicero, the poems of Virgil and Ovid, the plays of Terence, Plautus, and dialogues and letters composed in Latin and collected by the modern author Erasmus. This material was intended to help the boys think clearly and deeply about the world around them. It also acted as a model for their own speech and writing. Latin was the language of diplomacy, the law and learning, and no one could be thought of as educated who was ignorant of it. Shakespeare's plays and poems are filled with references to the Latin books he would have read and learned by heart at school.

But the grammar schools were educating boys for a new world in which their own language, English, was also being much more highly valued. It seems quite possible that both Richard Jenkins and John Cottom were influenced as teachers by one of the most radical and famous schoolmasters of the 16th century, Richard Mulcaster, who taught at the Merchant Taylor's school in London. It was Mulcaster's aim to do for the English language what traditional education did for Latin: to make young men confident in using their own language. He wrote: 'I love Rome, but London better. I favour Italy, but England more. I honour the Latin, but I worship the English.' Mulcaster's method had a second significant element. He believed that education was about confident use of the spoken word as well as the written language. And so he encouraged drama in his schools. His boys were to learn, through acting, the tricks of good, persuasive speech. This gave a particular energy to Mulcaster's system of education. Boys stood up, acting plays, scenes or dialogues in fresh modern English quite as much as they sat at desks studying their Latin texts.

Education in the grammar schools, then, was first and foremost about using language confidently and precisely. But it was very practical too. The skilled use of language would enable boys to be persuasive in their arguments, to win in disputes, to get their point of view across to others. Education was about rhetoric[†]: the art of persuasion.

This was nothing new. Rhetoric had always been part of the school curriculum. But its study had gained new impetus in the late 15th and 16th centuries. For instance, Rudolph Agricola wrote in 1479, 'The aim of language is to make someone share your own view... the speaker should be understood, the listener should be persuaded to listen eagerly... Grammar deals with the principles of correct and clear speech, rhetoric teaches us to be elegant and interesting in our speech – making traps for capturing ears.' The study of Latin authors was intended to give these skills. One big development in English education in the 16th century was that it showed how such techniques could be found in everyday language: in the conversations of the marketplace and the inn, or in the letters that were increasingly important means of communication. We will see how well Shakespeare learned these lessons. Throughout his plays and poems the tricks and traps of rhetoric are used to persuade, for good or ill.

31

CATHOLICS AND PROTESTANTS[†]

Throughout the 16th century, religion was one of the great dividing lines of English society. Once King Henry VIII provoked the final break with the Pope in 1534, English people had to choose between the old, Catholic, form of Christianity and the newer Protestant ways of belief and worship; the side they chose was also an indication of their political allegiance. Religious changes affected the whole of life.

Of course the changes were not simply the product of religious arguments. The growing power of merchants against that of the church, and the rise of independent nation-states, such as England, over and against the authority of the Pope, were preparing a fertile ground for the new order. But the crucial test of which side you were on was a religious one.

These religious arguments spilled into the life of Stratford in a number of very typical ways. First, the system of government, which had been closely linked with the church, was changed. The Guild of the Holy Cross was replaced by the Corporation of bailiff and aldermen. Second, the outward show of religious and social life was altered. Church services began to be in English, not Latin. Clergymen began to marry. The richly decorated churches became bare and simple. In January 1564, John Shakespeare, chamberlain of the town, paid workmen two shillings 'for defacing images in the Chapel'. The wall-paintings in the Guild Chapel, once the home of the Guild of the Holy Cross and now the place where town officials worshipped, were hidden behind a coat of whitewash, which was not removed until 1804.

It is interesting that Stratford was late in taking this action. The government in London had ordered such things to be done four years earlier. The Guild Chapel paintings were covered over, not destroyed as the government expected. Perhaps many Stratford citizens were keen to see the return of Catholicism as the religion of England.

John Shakespeare himself may have been one of these recusants[†], as they were called (from the Latin word *recuso*, I refuse). He may have played less of a part in town life after 1577 because he was sympathetic to Catholicism. Certainly by the 1590s he was staying away from church – an offence for which he was fined. Many Stratford families and some of the extended Shakespeare family were Catholic, including some Ardens. When William Shakespeare's Catholic cousin, John Somerville, was arrested in 1583, he was on his way to assassinate the queen. None of this proves absolutely that John Shakespeare was a Catholic. He might have stayed away from church because he was in debt and was afraid of arrest. He may have ceased to be part of town life because of the decline in his business. But opinion now tends to the view that he had Catholic sympathies, and this has lent weight to theories about what happened to William Shakespeare in the years between leaving school in about 1580 and his arrival in London sometime before 1592 – the so-called lost years.

THE LOST YEARS

We know that William Shakespeare married Anne Hathaway of Shottery, near Stratford, in November 1582. She was eight years older than him. They

33

married in haste, by special licence, presumably because she was already pregnant with their first child, Susanna, who was baptized in May 1583. Two years later William and Anne had twins, Judith and Hamnet, baptized in January 1585. But that is all we know for certain of those years.

Some of Shakespeare's biographers have implied that there is a yawning gap in the great man's life – a gap to be filled with wild speculation. Maybe he was a soldier and went abroad, or he trained as a lawyer; perhaps he trained as a schoolmaster or acted as private tutor in the household of a rich family. There are stories of how he poached deer at Charlecote a few miles east of Stratford. There are drinking stories and travelling stories. And they are all good stories – but there is no hard evidence to back any of them up.

Over the years, however, one group of ideas has begun to cluster together into a story which some scholars think may account for these lost years. The stories link William's obvious intelligence, the possibility of learning to be an actor, and his father's likely Catholicism. Many people think they ring more true than most of the other theories.

Briefly the story is this. Remember John Cottom, the Catholic schoolmaster who went back to Lancashire in 1581? What if he thought highly of the bright boy from a Catholic family he had taught in Stratford and recommended him to nearby Catholic families, the Hoghtons and the Heskeths? So William arrives in Lancashire as a schoolmaster but one who already has the acting bug. (We know that companies of players visited Stratford during his childhood.) Soon he is involved with the Hoghton family's own troupe of players. In August 1581 Alexander Hoghton's will refers to a servant called William Shakeshafte (a not impossible version of Shakespeare's name: names were often spelt in different ways at this time). Is that the Stratford boy?

The story requires us to think that Shakespeare was back in Stratford between 1582 and 1585. During those years he married and had three children. Then with a wife and three children to support, and no doubt with ambitions to satisfy, he decides to seek his fortune again as a player and playwright. He joins a company of players with strong connections with the same Lancashire Catholic families he had been working for: Lord Strange's Men. We know that many of the other players in this acting company later became Shakespeare's close and lifelong colleagues in the Lord Chamberlain's Men and the King's Men.

All of this is speculation, but it does bring together some of the known facts of Shakespeare's life, and makes sense of others. However, it does require us to believe, first, that by the age of 17 he was so established as a player that he could be referred to in Alexander Hoghton's will; second, that having got himself into this position he then effectively gave it up to move back to Stratford, get married and have three children; and third, that he then rejoined a company of actors and worked with them in London, where he also began to write.

The argument may seem plausible – but it is not the only possibility. Shakespeare may have remained in Stratford, working with his father perhaps, or even assisting at his old school, married Anne Hathaway and had his children. There would have been plenty of opportunities to see companies of players in Stratford – there were frequent performances in the Guild Hall. In June 1587 one of the best companies, the Queen's Men, had a problem. One of their actors, William Knell, had been killed in a duel at Thame in Oxfordshire. We don't know whether they were on their way to Stratford or had just left, but it is possible that Shakespeare, either as a young hopeful – or as an already experienced actor (if the Lancashire link is correct) – joined them.

By the late 1580s or early 1590s Shakespeare had arrived on the London scene as a player and playwright. However he got there, he must somehow have learned his trade and convinced others of his skill. So one element that goes to make up the so-called lost years is presumably some sort of apprenticeship[†] with a company of players. This may have been through Lord Strange's Men or through the Queen's Men, or a combination of both. What we do know is that the lost years come to an end in 1592 when a dying playwright called Robert Greene attacked a new writer who had been replacing him in popularity. Greene sarcastically tells other established playwrights to beware

> 'an upstart Crow, beautified with our feathers that... supposes he is as well able to bombast out a blank verse as the rest of you and... is in his own conceit the only Shake-scene in a country... O that I might entreat your rare wits to be imploied in more profitable courses... I knowe the best husband of you will never prove a Usuer and the kindest of them all will never prove a kind nurse...'

Greene's attack tells us four important things about

this writer: that he is popular; that he is a mere player – his writing has been learned on the job, not at the universities; that he is a money-lender ('I know the best husband of you will never prove a Usurer [money-lender]'); and that he is William Shakespeare – 'the only Shake-scene in a country'. By 1592, then, William Shakespeare had worked out his apprenticeship as a player and begun to write plays popular enough to replace those of Robert Greene. He may have been linked with the Queen's Men or Lord Strange's Men, or both (Greene's plays were being replaced in the repertoires of both those companies by Shakespeare's during the early 1590s). Most interesting of all, he may have arrived in London continuing his father's business. We know that John Shakespeare was a money-lender as well as a glover, and traded in a range of goods. Every ambitious merchant needed a London connection. We will see that William Shakespeare, as well as pursuing his own career, kept business connections with Stratford. Perhaps he did so from the beginning.

3
THE BEGINNINGS OF DRAMA

The impulse to tell stories is as old as humanity. Performing stories and watching others act them out is one of the most basic social activities.

For the Ancient Greeks, drama was an outpouring of the dangerous power of the god Dionysus. This might take the form of rough, even improvised performances at crucial moments like seedtime and harvest, weddings or funerals, or it might be a highly ritualized, skilfully acted and carefully prepared event attended by all the citizens of a town. Either way, the aim was ecstasy: actors and onlookers alike were taken out of themselves, lifted up by the power of the god into terror, or delight: in the mirror of the stage they saw themselves as they might wish – or fear – to be.

Plays were performed to mark the change of seasons, or the important moments in human life, or to remember the defining moments in the history of a village, a city or a nation. Drama told stories to help communities understand who they were and where they had come from. The performances helped people take responsibility for their lives and play their part in dealing with the unexpected.

Finally, drama was an outpouring of energy. It was never dull. Dramatic performances were like carnivals: dangerous, emotionally exhausting events. They were tidal waves sweeping along individuals and whole communities.

FOLK DRAMA

The Ancient Greek experience reminds us that drama

begins with the worship of gods. Even after the reasons for telling this story or doing that dance have been forgotten, the event itself remains in village festivals or increasingly obscure rituals. England in the Middle Ages was full of such festivals, and many of them have lasted to the present day. The Abbot's Bromley Horn in Staffordshire, for example, is a dance for a group of men who wear ancient sets of deer-antlers as they dance through their village. The Furry Dance in Helston and the Padstow Hobby dance, both in Cornwall, still draw crowds although their true purpose is almost forgotten. There are sword dancers, morris dancers and maypole dancers; wells are 'dressed' with flowers in Derbyshire. Towns and villages still have fairs or carnivals which date back to the worship of pre-Christian gods. Many of the dances include mock-fights which originally acted out the battle between winter and summer, or between rival tribes. Other dances have links with fertility: the need to make crops grow or to bring the sexes together and start a new generation to ensure village life goes on. Some of these events took the form of plays, performed by mummers† or guisers†, often about Robin Hood or St George. We know that in the 16th century the people of Stratford watched a play every year about St George and the Dragon.

These plays had all the elements of combat, death and rebirth and ended with a sword dance. They are one of the many bits of raw material that go into the hugely energetic plays of Shakespeare and his contemporaries. Shakespeare's plays often end with a bawdy, sexually suggestive dance, and sometimes there are clear links to the cycles of nature. The comedy *Love's Labour's*

Lost ends with two songs, one about winter, the other about summer. *A Midsummer Night's Dream* ends with a bergamasque† danced by the countrymen who have just performed at the wedding banquet. Even when not written in, and however alien to the mood of the play, it seems that audiences expected a dance. We know that a performance of *Julius Caesar* in 1599 ended with just such a jig†, an opportunity for the clowns to do their stuff.

DRAMA AND THE CHURCH

There has always been a close connection between drama and religion. We have seen that many folk traditions began as celebrations of pre-Christian gods. The growth of Christianity transferred some of these into the church. Christmas celebrations began as festivals at the turn of the year, when the sun began to climb back towards summer. Easter eggs are ancient symbols of fertility. Church services are themselves dramas that tell the story of the death and resurrection of Jesus Christ. As they developed in magnificence and complexity, some other short plays grew out of them and began to stand alone. One of the first was enacted early on the morning of Easter Day and showed the women finding the tomb of Jesus empty.

In 1311 the Church established a new festival which was to become crucial to the development of drama, not only in England but right across Europe. Some years earlier, theologians had finally formulated a new understanding of the body and blood of Christ which worshippers receive at the Holy Communion or Mass. They wanted to stress the miraculous way in which what was human became divine, how the bread and wine placed on the altar became Christ's body and blood. The Feast of Corpus Christi[†] (from the Latin words meaning 'the Body of Christ') was established to present this doctrine to Christians. The new understanding required a new 'drama' that would emphasize Christ's humanity and at the same time be a celebration of the human story.

By the middle of the 14th century in many countries, and in many English towns, cycles of plays had been developed which told the story of God's dealings with the human race from the beginning to the end of history. The plays were deliberately a celebration, too, of humanity; through them the characters in the Bible stories became recognizable human beings. Costume, speech, settings and characters were local – the aim of the plays was to show those who enacted them, as well as those who watched and heard them, that characters in the Bible stories to whom God had appeared were no different from themselves and their neighbours. Shepherds in the fields outside Bethlehem complain about the taxman in Yorkshire accents. Carpenters use real hammers and nails to pin Jesus onto the cross.

As well as the obvious religious teaching provided by these cycles of plays, they had at least three other characteristics. First, the plays were written in English, and were produced and performed by local people. Each play was the responsibility of a particular group – often the guilds[†] (or mysteries[†] – hence the term 'mystery play' often used for these dramas) of craftsmen or merchants. Preparing and performing the dramas was an event in which the whole community joined. Second, in the plays the everyday became a subject of drama showing God's involvement here and now with human life. They gave scope for showing, with wit and pathos, the ordinary lives of men and women in the towns where they were performed. And third, the mystery plays encouraged the development of the whole range of drama skills. People learned how to write dialogue and construct plots, create sets, costumes and props, and players began to understand how to portray character and work an audience.

In England the Corpus Christi plays continued until 1548 when the theological changes in the English church after the break with Rome led to their abolition. They were revived again when Catholicism[†] was restored under Queen Mary (queen from 1553 to 1558), but with her death and the return of the Protestant[†] religion they were once more abolished. The very last performance (until modern times) of any of the English cycles was in Coventry in 1580. Coventry is just a few miles from Stratford. Was the 16-year-old William Shakespeare there to watch? We don't know, but it is possible, especially if his family were secretly Catholics. What we do know, however, is that the mystery cycles lived on in the energy, in the love of plays about ordinary men and women, and in the whole range of designing, making and acting skills of the theatre of which Shakespeare was to be a part.

POWER AND DISPLAY

One of the most effective ways in which the church communicated not only its message but also its power over the lives of men and women was by the magnificence of its ceremonies. Priests, and especially bishops and popes, wore expensive liturgical costume, encrusted with jewels and wonderfully embroidered. The churches within which they acted out these ceremonies were usually amongst the largest buildings in a town and contained beautiful carvings and majestic stained-glass windows. Worshippers were intended to be over-awed by the power of God as represented by his Church on Earth.

Kings and princes – and later on in the Middle Ages, merchants and town or city councils – trying in their own way to impress the people, took their cue from the Church. The relationships between king and sub-ject or between cities had to be shown and acted out. Processions and pageants[†] – dramatic displays – showed a city's wealth and power just as much as its great buildings did.

The need to establish power relationships was never far away, and during the 16th century what has been called 'the liturgy of state' gradually overtook the litur-gies (services) of the Church in splendour and impor-tance. When King James I processed through London in March 1604, the whole event was a carefully con-structed piece of flattery. Temporary archways had been built along the route, carved with symbols of the new king's wisdom and power. The procession was brought to a halt here and there while companies of actors performed in the king's honour.

The procession through London was a localized form of another important royal event, the progress[†], in which monarchs travelled through the country showing themselves to the people and receiving tributes. In July 1575, Queen Elizabeth I visited Kenilworth Castle, a few miles north of Stratford. Kenilworth was the home of the Earl of Leicester, an important nobleman who, it

RICHARD TARLTON.

From a drawing of the same Size in the Pepysian Library at Magdalen College

Pub. April 20 1792, by R.H. nd in g Fleet Street

An 18th century copy of John Scottowe's drawing of Richard Tarlton, the player and clown, who died in 1588.

44

is now thought, was trying to persuade the queen to marry him. Leicester provided the queen and her court (a progress involved a large number of people) with three weeks of entertainment, including firework displays, hunting and bear-baiting, and plays and pageants, many of which took place outdoors in the woods and by the lake at the castle. There was a comic country wedding for the queen to enjoy, and a magnificent water-pageant. Robert Langham, a court official who was present, described the events surrounding the queen's visit to Kenilworth in a mock-serious letter a year later. He writes how, in the pageant,

> 'Harry Goldingham was to represent Arion upon the Dolphin's back, but finding his voice to be very hoarse and unpleasant, he tears off his disguise and swears he was none of Arion, not he, but honest Harry Goldingham: which blunt discovery pleased the Queen better than if it had gone through the right way.'

In 1575, Shakespeare was 11 years old and it is possible that he, with many others, may have gone to the castle grounds to marvel at the festivities.

Great noblemen like the Earl of Leicester had a long tradition of employing groups of actors to provide entertainments for the household and its visitors. We have already seen that Shakespeare himself may have worked with such a company in Lancashire as a young man. When they were not performing for their employer, or travelling between London and the country estates he owned, the companies performed in other towns and villages. We know that Stratford had many visits from such companies during the 16th century. In fact the Earl of Leicester's Men themselves played in the Guild Hall in Stratford in 1573 when

John Shakespeare was an alderman[†] and William was nine years old. Was he taken by his father to see them? And was this the beginning of it all?

Queen Elizabeth I also had her company of actors. In 1583, the courtier responsible for performances, the Lord Chamberlain[†] (at that time, Sir Francis Walsingham), instructed his assistant, the Master of the Revels[†], to put together a company of players made up of the best men from the other companies. The Queen's Men were not tied to performances before the queen, but they were under her protection and were a privileged group. Their links with the queen, however, gave rise at times to some confusion. There is a story that when the Queen's Men were playing in Norfolk, the playgoers began to laugh when the company's clown, Richard Tarlton, stuck his head round the curtain (no doubt pulling a face). At this an officer of the law started to tell the audience off: their laughter was showing a lack of respect for the queen's livery, which the actors were wearing.

This story neatly shows the ambivalence about plays and playing which has always been at the heart of the theatre profession. We have seen that drama is both an energetic overturning of expectations – the unruly power of the god Dionysus is never far away – and it is also a means of displaying power and authority. Are plays carefully controlled expressions of religious or political power and players merely servants of the state, or are they anarchic explosions – carnivals of the human spirit? We shall see as we now turn to the rise of the playing companies during the 16th century, and William Shakespeare's role in them, that this problem was never far from the surface.

4
THE RISE OF THE PLAYING COMPANIES

Throughout the 16th century, plays were part of the ferment of ideas and growing unrest caused by rapid social, political and religious changes. As well as using drama to show their power, rulers were also finding it necessary to ban plays and control players. The mystery cycles[†] were suppressed, for example – it was felt that as the products of Catholicism[†] they could be a focus for unrest at a time when Catholic sympathizers were seen as the state's enemies. Cities such as Coventry, Lincoln and Norwich, which had been the home of the great mystery cycles, now became (by the 1540s) centres for troupes of players who continued to travel around the country, part of an increasingly restless population which the government took steps to control. In May 1545, King Henry VIII proclaimed that not only 'ruffians and vagabonds' but also those 'common players' to be found on the south bank of the Thames (where Shakespeare's Globe theatre would stand just over 50 years later) were to be forced into the Navy.

There were increasingly harsh laws against uncontrolled plays throughout the 1550s, and many players risked imprisonment or worse for performances which increased the political and religious tension of the times. Playing required a licence, and companies attached to guilds[†] or towns could not survive.

ROGUES AND VAGABONDS

The attempt to control players by making them the servants of noblemen reached its climax in the Act for the Punishment of Rogues, Vagabonds and Sturdy

Beggars of 1572. This Act was intended primarily to prevent anyone arrested as a vagrant or beggar from claiming that they were players and so avoid punishment. It effectively limited companies of players from wandering from town to town or from one great house to another in search of an audience. The Act stated, in the legal language of the time, that

'all idle persons goinge aboute in any Countrie, either begginge, or usinge any subtile Crafte or unlawfull Games and Playes... all Fencers Bearwardes common Players of Enterludes [plays] and Minstrels wandringe abroad (other than Players of Enterludes belonginge to any Baron of this Realme, or any other honourable Personage of greater Degree...) shalbe taken adjudged and deemed as Rogues Vagabondes and Sturdie Beggers, and shall suffer such Paine and Punishment as in the saide Acte is in that behalfe appointed...'

Other legislation also tightened the link between players and their patron†, the lord of whose household they were a part. Plays were subject to censorship (the text had to be approved by officials of the church and state before it could be performed) and the patron had to take some of the responsibility when they were deemed unacceptable. Finally, the patron needed royal permission for his players. Queen Elizabeth never forgot that players were powerful weapons in the hands of traitorous noblemen, and might stir up dangerous unrest throughout the towns and villages of England.

LEICESTER'S MEN

In 1574, two years after the Act for the Punishment of Rogues, Vagabonds and Sturdy Beggars, a company of players wanted to have their situation secured. The Earl of Leicester, one of the most powerful men in

England, had kept a company of players for many years. Now they wrote and asked that he would

'vouchsafe to retain us as your household servants... not that we mean to crave any further stipend or benefit at your lordship's hand but your liveries as we have had, and also your Honour's licence to certify that we are your household servants when we shall have occasion to travel among our friends as we do usually once a year and as other nobleman's players do and have done in times past.'

Shortly after, the Earl of Leicester's Men received the royal licence. It is worth quoting at length, because it effectively lays down the rules for the development of the theatre in which Shakespeare was to flourish.

Five named players (James Burbage, John Perkyn, John Laneham, William Johnson and Robert Wilson) were given permission

'to use, exercise and occupy the art and faculty of playing comedies, tragedies interludes stage plays and such other like... as well within our City of London and liberties of the same as also within the liberties and freedoms of any of our cities towns boroughs etc as without the same... provided the said comedies [etc] must be seen by the Master of our Revels... before seen and allowed and that the same be not published or shewen in the time of common prayer or in the time of great and common plague in our said city of London.'

The letter and the licence give a number of important indications about the development of players' companies. First, they were self-supporting: they looked to their patron for both support and influence at court, but otherwise they took financial responsibility (and shared the profits between them). Second, they went on tour, at least for some weeks each year. Third, they had a range of plays to perform but they all had to be approved by an officer of the queen. Fourth, the licence covered each player separately: they could set up alone, hire other actors and travel independently – so long as they obeyed the terms of the licence. And fifth, they could play anywhere, and at any time except during church service times and outbreaks of the plague†. This had two major implications for the Shakespearean theatre. Daily performances meant they needed a place of their own in which to play. But the royal permission to play in London as well as in its Liberties† (those areas outside the control of the city authorities, such as Shoreditch to the north and Bankside to the south) was to lead to constant controversies with those who thought plays were a risk to health (spreading the plague) and morality (spreading treason or lust or general disorder). The stage was being set not only for the creation of theatres such as The Globe, but also for the battle with the Puritans† which would eventually shut the theatres in 1642.

STRATFORD AND LONDON

We have seen in the previous chapter that William Shakespeare may have been living in Lancashire in 1581. If he is the William Shakeshafte referred to in the will of Alexander Hoghton and afterwards taken under the wing of Sir Thomas Hesketh, then he was one of a company of actors and musicians. It is possible that after Alexander Hoghton's death, Hesketh was able to place Shakespeare with another acting company (Lord Strange's Men) whom we will come to shortly. Or he may have returned to Stratford during the summer of 1582.

Certainly by 1582 John Shakespeare was in financial

difficulties. In the years after 1578 he began to borrow money on the security of his wife's estate. In November 1582 William married Anne Hathaway, already pregnant with their first child. Further children (twins) were born in 1585. With other brothers able to keep the gloving business going, presumably William began to consider his options.

London, then as now, was the place to be. If William had already had some links with powerful families, he could pick them up again in the city. If he wanted to pursue a career as a writer or player, London was where the theatres were. And if he went to London he could provide the family business with important trade contacts.

THE QUEEN'S MEN

During the 1570s a number of companies followed a similar pattern to Leicester's Men. The Earl of Essex's Men, Oxford's, Pembroke's, Warwick's and the Earl of Derby's Men, for example, toured around the country in the summer – perhaps on their way to or from their patrons' country houses – and found a place to perform in London for the rest of the year.

We know that a company known as the Queen's Men played in Stratford in the summer of 1569, when John Shakespeare was bailiff[†], and William just five years old. But that company seems to have been disbanded until, in 1583, Sir Francis Walsingham, as Lord Chamberlain[†] responsible for court entertainments, requested Sir Edmund Tilney, the Master of the Revels[†], to choose the 12 most accomplished players from the other companies and create the Queen's Men. This company was rather different from the others in at least three ways: first, the players do not appear to have been sharers[†] – they were not really a business partnership; second, they agreed only to perform as the Queen's Men – unlike other players they could not 'do their own thing' or join other companies; and third, they were allowed to play in the city of London without interference from the city authorities, who were beginning to clamp down hard on the playing companies.

The Queen's Men were the most important company for the next five years. They included three of the founding players of Leicester's Men (Laneham, Wilson and Johnson), and one of their clowns, Richard Tarlton, was among the most famous performers of his day. They went out on tour just like the other companies. In the summer of 1587 they were at Thame in Oxfordshire when one of their players, William Knell, was killed in a fight. Knell was famous in serious roles and his death must have been a blow to the company. The Queen's Men were also in Stratford during that summer, though it is impossible to say whether this was before or after the death of Knell. But some scholars have suggested that the young William Shakespeare may have joined them at this stage – not to take on Knell's roles, but to make up the numbers of a depleted company. If he had already acted with Lord Hoghton's company of players in Lancashire, then perhaps he had experience enough to be an attractive prospect. Certainly some of Shakespeare's later plays are reworkings of plays that were in the Queen's Men's repertoire – maybe this is when he learned them.

Whether or not the Queen's Men included the

23-year-old William Shakespeare among their numbers when they returned to London in the late autumn
of 1587, their glory days were soon over. Much of
their success seems to have been built on the antics of
their famous clown Richard Tarlton. Once Tarlton
died in September 1588 the Queen's Men quickly
declined and many of the players began to transfer to
other companies.

JOHN HEMINGES

The records suggest that it was common for groups of
players to transfer their allegiance together. The case
of John Heminges illustrates this, and may also give us
an insight into what may have happened to William
Shakespeare if he had been with the Queen's Men
from 1587.

On 10 March 1588, Heminges married Rebecca, the
widow of the murdered William Knell. This suggests
that Heminges too was associated with the Queen's
Men. We know that by 1593 he was a member of
another company, Lord Strange's Men, and a year
later was, with William Shakespeare, a founder of the
Lord Chamberlain's Men. John Heminges and
William Shakespeare continued their association until
the latter's death in 1616 – and beyond, for Heminges
(together with Henry Condell, another player whose
pedigree may be traced back at least to 1593, and
possibly 1590, with Lord Strange's Men) edited and
published the collected edition of Shakespeare's plays
in 1623. Indeed, with Lord Strange's Men we are on
altogether firmer ground for signs of Shakespeare.
There is strong evidence that he was associated with
this company at least from 1589. Maybe he joined

them at the same time as other former Queen's Men, although some scholars think that he was in fact with Lord Strange's Men from about 1582, spending only short periods of time in Stratford.

LORD STRANGE'S MEN

Ferdinando, Lord Strange, was the eldest son of the fourth Earl of Derby – another of the great Lancashire Catholic families. Lord Strange kept a company of players throughout the 1580s, but it was their amalgamation with the Admiral's Men (patron: Lord Howard of Effingham, Lord Admiral since 1585) and the arrival of Edward Alleyn into the company in 1589 which really put them on the map.

Alleyn was one of the greatest players of the Elizabethan stage. Two years younger than Shakespeare, by the time he was in his mid-twenties he had become famous for his ability to play big and energetic roles – especially those in the plays of Christopher Marlowe.

CHRISTOPHER MARLOWE AND THE UNIVERSITY WITS

Playwriting was the preserve of two distinct groups at this time. Many players produced material – often comedies – geared to the tastes of their audience. Other plays were written by university men. Some were schoolmasters, writing for their pupils according to the educational principles of the day. In 1527 the boys of St Paul's School in London performed the Latin comedy *Menaechmi*, written by Plautus. By the 1550s Nicholas Udall, headmaster of Eton School, had written *Ralph Roister Doister*, a comedy that

Edward Alleyn (1566–1626), one of the greatest actors of his day.
This portrait now hangs in Dulwich College, London, the school
he founded in 1616.

successfully marries Latin models with energetic English language and characterization. Other writers educated at Cambridge or Oxford used the English language for tragedies†, again often following Latin models, for performances at the universities or at court.

By the 1580s, university educated writers were also providing plays for the companies. Some were delicate comedies, full of fantasy and the supernatural, with serious undercurrents. For example, John Lyly's *Campaspe* of 1584 is described as 'A tragical comedie' and the mixture of styles is even more pronounced in George Peele's *The Old Wives' Tale* (1591). Lyly and Peele wrote for highly professional companies of boy players†, but another university man, Robert Greene, made his mark with the adult companies – probably including the Queen's Men and Lord Strange's Men – with such plays as *James the Fourth*, about Scottish courtly intrigue, and *Friar Bacon and Friar Bungay*, which mixes up clowning and romance in ways not unlike those we will see later in Shakespeare.

Without doubt the greatest of the university educated playwrights was Christopher Marlowe. Marlowe was a rebel, and his plays burn with anger, wit, irreverence and defiance like none before. In *Tamburlaine* (written about 1587) he paints a sweeping picture of a world conqueror achieving greatness before falling like a burned-out rocket. *Doctor Faustus* (written about 1587) makes a pact with the devil for greatness and loses his life and his soul, while *The Jew of Malta* (written about 1589) is a portrait of all-consuming evil succumbing not to goodness, but to greater, political, cunning. Marlowe's plays focus on a great man rising

56

above the world around him and conquering by fire or sword or wickedness before drowning in the very seas of blood he has created. They have the energy of those battles between good and evil found in the religious plays of the mystery cycles – but goodness has almost disappeared from his world of cunning politicians, wily devils and scheming courtiers. The central characters (always named in the titles, until the last – *The Massacre at Paris* – which dramatizes recent events in France) are much larger than life and needed an exceptional player to bring them off. In Edward Alleyn, Lord Strange's Men found just the man.

Marlowe's plays were a huge and scandalous success. He showed how the public theatres could tackle big themes with intelligence, flair and a good deal of showmanship. His plays were noisy, energetic spectacles which nevertheless explored complex political and moral issues. If, as seems most likely, Shakespeare was by now acting with Lord Strange's Men and establishing himself as a writer, from such plays as these he learned his craft.

5

THE ONELY SHAKE-SCENE IN A COUNTREY

However he got there – whether with the Queen's Men or Lord Strange's Men – by 1592 William Shakespeare was part of the London theatre scene. Whichever company of players gave him a start, by now he was almost certainly engaged with Lord Strange's Men, making a name for himself as a player and playwright and, like all successful people, inevitably making enemies as well.

In September 1592 a pamphlet appeared, said to have been written on his deathbed by the playwright Robert Greene. The author of the pamphlet, *Greene's Groatsworth of Wit*, makes a number of accusations against another writer, who had formerly been an acquaintance if not a friend, but who now had failed to help him in his time of need. The passage is well known, but is still worth quoting:

> 'there is an upstart Crow, beautified with our feathers, that with his Tygers hart wrapt in a Players hyde, supposes he is as well able to bombast out a blank verse as the best of you: and beeing an absolute *Johannes fac totum*, is in his owne conceit the onely Shake-scene in a countrey... O that I might intreat your rare wits to be imploied in more profitable courses... I knowe the best husband of you will never prove a Usurer and the kindest of them all will never prove a kind nurse...'

There is plenty of internal evidence to tell us that whoever wrote this pamphlet was attacking Shakespeare. He parodies a line from one of Shakespeare's earliest plays, *The True Tragedy of Richard, Duke of York, and the Death of Good King Henry the Sixth...* (usually known nowadays as *Henry VI Part 3*) where the Duke of York refers to Queen Margaret as a 'tiger's heart wrapped in a woman's hide'. And 'Shake-scene' clinches it – who else but 'Shakespeare'?

The attack gives us much more information, though, which may help to draw a picture of Shakespeare as seen by his contemporaries in 1592. First, the author directs his warnings about 'Shake-scene' to writers who, like himself, were university educated men. They had written plays for the boy companies[†], the Queen's Men and/or Lord Strange's Men but here was a newcomer – 'an upstart Crow' – outdoing them at their own game – 'beautified with our feathers'. He was a player turned playwright – '*Johannes fac totum*' (Latin for 'Jack of all trades') – who by his success was condemning the established writers to poverty. Presumably Shakespeare's radical experiments had made Greene's plays – and Lyly's and Peele's – no longer fashionable. But there is more. The author of the pamphlet accuses 'Shake-scene' of arrogance – 'in his owne conceit the onely Shake-scene in a countrey' – and finally refers to him as a usurer, a money-lender, who would not help Greene in his distress, but who hoards his money for his own purposes.

We might be tempted to dismiss the attack as a bad case of sour grapes, but behind the invective hides a realistic picture which we will find repeated throughout Shakespeare's life. We should remember that by the early 1580s John Shakespeare had fallen on hard times. All merchants needed to be able to borrow and lend money at different times and he did both. At times he even lived in fear of being arrested for debt. But by 1596 he is referred to as a man of wealth. William must have used his own success as a player (much better paid than as a playwright) to remake the family fortunes, acquiring wealth and property along the way.

THE FIRST PLAYS

We do not know for sure when Shakespeare began to write plays. Some scholars think that none of the plays later collected into the Folio[†] of 1623 was written before about 1590; others would date the earliest to 1587 or 1588. Four pieces of evidence support the earlier dates.

1. The attack in *Greene's Groatsworth of Wit* shows a man already successful and well-known. Surely this must be built on more than two years' worth of playwriting?

2. In 1614, Shakespeare's great play-writing contemporary Ben Jonson, in his play *Bartholomew Fair*, refers to Shakespeare's *Titus Andronicus* as having been written 'some twenty-five or thirty years' earlier. This would date it to between 1584 and 1589. While 1584 does seem rather too early – the grasp of dramatic technique is surely too assured for a 20-year-old writer – 1589 or a little earlier would be quite possible.

3. The title page of the printed edition of *Titus Andronicus* (1594) tells us that it had already been performed by three companies. The closure of the theatres throughout most of 1593 meant that companies had gone 'on the road'. It appears that a group of Lord Strange's Men separated from the main company and toured as the Earl of Pembroke's Men. By September 1593 they were bankrupt and sold some plays, either to printers or to other companies. *Titus*

Andronicus was one of these. Presumably Pembroke's Men had taken a play already well established in their repertoire with them when they separated from Lord Strange's Men and now sold it to another company to help pay off their debts.

4. In the early play *The Two Gentlemen of Verona*, the comic character Launce has a dog. It is just possible that the role was played by, or written for, the great clown Richard Tarlton, whom we know had a performing dog. Tarlton died in 1588. We know of no other clown at the time with a performing dog and the play seems never to have been performed again during Shakespeare's lifetime. Did the play die with Tarlton? If so, it may have been written for him, and the Queen's Men, in or before 1588.

The Two Gentlemen of Verona shifts the gentle love-comedies of John Lyly from the boys' companies into the world of adult players, with a corresponding raising of tension and emotional range. Proteus and Valentine are good friends. Proteus is loved by Julia. When Valentine leaves Verona for another Italian town, Milan, Proteus decides to follow him. His friendship for Valentine is greater than his love for Julia. But in Milan both young men fall in love with the same woman, Silvia. Towards the end of the play Proteus rescues Silvia who has been captured by outlaws. But she is still not safe because Proteus threatens to rape her. Fortunately Valentine is hiding nearby, sees what his former friend is trying to do, and stops him. Proteus has shown himself a poor friend to Valentine, betrayed the love Julia feels for him and threatened an innocent woman. Good friendship and true love turn bad. Even the closest relationships are fragile. The play resolves itself quickly and not altogether convincingly: Valentine forgives Proteus, who hands over Silvia. A pageboy turns out to be Julia in disguise. She is reunited with Proteus and all ends more happily than Proteus's behaviour perhaps deserves. But even in such an early play many typically Shakespearean themes are present. Throughout his career he was to track the intricate paths of love and friendship, to make great use of disguise, and, in the clowns Launce and Speed, to allow a comic sub-plot to mirror and illuminate the moral and psychological worlds of the central characters. Although rarely performed, the play has wonderfully funny scenes and the verse in which the lovers speak is full of wit and insight. Above all, Shakespeare has already learned to show, and not just to tell, us his stories.

The Taming of the Shrew is almost certainly another very early play. Where *The Two Gentlemen of Verona* explored the rhetoric† of friendship, using balanced and repetitive verse to show the shifting feelings of the lovers, *The Shrew* examines the power games below the surface of love and marriage. Already the gap between truth and appearance is opening; the suspicion that words may not mean what they say is taking hold.

The plot is complex: three plots intertwine and illuminate one other. First, as a frame to the play, the drunken Christopher Sly is tricked into thinking he is a lord for whom a play is to be performed. That play has two layers: the wooing the shrewish (bad-tempered, foul-mouthed) Katherine by Petruccio, on the look-out for a rich wife; and the attempts of Lucentio, Gremio and Hortensio to marry Katherine's sister, Bianca. The play has stock characters and set-piece scenes reminiscent of the Italian *Commedia*† tradition and is a hilarious knockabout farce†. But there is a serious undercurrent. Bianca's suitors see it as a business venture, although protesting they love her. Petruccio treats Katherine's wooing like a business deal, but seems to transform her into a loving wife.

Near the end of the play the men bet on who will be the most obedient wife. To everyone's surprise, Katherine wins and then makes a long speech telling women that husbands should be the lords and masters of their wives:

> Thy husband is thy lord, thy life, thy keeper,
> Thy head, thy sovereign, one that cares for thee...
> And craves no other tribute at thy hands
> But love, fair looks, and true obedience...
> Such duty as the subject owes the prince,
> Even such a woman oweth to her husband...'
>
> The Taming of the Shrew, Act 5 Scene 2, lines 151–2, 157–8, 160–1

This speech might appear preposterous, even offensive, today but when performed it can give a very different impression to that of the printed page.

We might accept that Katherine is simply stating the beliefs of her day, and the speech could be played that way. But actresses playing Katherine today often make other choices. After the speech, Petruccio seems surprised ('Why, there's a wench!'). Perhaps Katherine has decided to be like her husband – subverting expectations, shocking those around her, being a free spirit like Petruccio. Or maybe Katherine accepts that this is the public role of a wife, but in private things can be very different – husbands and wives rely on one another in ways the world never sees, they become a team. Or again, maybe she knows that Petruccio has laid a bet on her obedience, and plays the game with him – once more, the two of them against the world. The number of choices available to a player here remind us that we should take nothing at face value in a Shakespeare play: there is always a gap between appearance and reality, and the truth is more likely to be found dancing like an electric charge between many options than fixed down with clear certainty.

With his next two plays, written probably in 1590–91, Shakespeare broke new ground. He explored the history of England as it collapsed into civil war under King Henry VI in the middle of the 15th century. *The First Part of the Contention of the Two Famous Houses of York and Lancaster with the Death of the Good Duke Humphrey* (known in most editions as *Henry VI Part 2*, and here as *The Contention*) looks at the ten years between 1445 and 1455 as a weak king struggled unsuccessfully against his nobles. Richard, Duke of York, tries to overthrow Henry by manipulating a peasant rebellion led by Jack Cade, and, as the play closes, seems about to take the throne.

The True Tragedy of Richard, Duke of York and the Death of Good King Henry the Sixth (*Henry VI Part 3*) picks up the story. Richard is killed early on and the play focuses on his sons' struggle with Queen Margaret, Henry's wife, for control of the country. *The True Tragedy* ends with Henry and his son murdered by the Yorkists; Edward, Earl of March (Richard's son) on the throne as Edward IV; and another son, Richard, Duke of Gloucester, beginning to prepare his own murderous way to the throne.

Shakespeare relied extensively on Raphael Holinshed's *Chronicles*, a history of the time printed in 1587, but the plays skilfully manipulate history in order to reveal political and personal ambitions being played out on the battlefield of England. They are bold sweeping epics where armies march and countermarch, murders are committed and avenged, and much blood is spilt. But there are also many complex characterizations: the saintly Henry VI, shocked by the civil war being waged about him; the scheming Richard of Gloucester; the power politics of the Earl of Warwick. There are also many small but beautifully crafted roles: George, Duke of Clarence, the brother of Edward and Richard; Lady Grey, who will marry King Edward; a soldier who has killed his son; another soldier who has killed his father. Shakespeare paints a picture in which battles between the rival noble houses of Lancaster and York tear England apart from top to bottom. At the end Margaret is banished to France and King Edward proclaims a time of peace, but the very last line of the play sounds a note of foreboding.

'For here, I hope, begins our lasting joy.'

We have already been given an insight into Richard of Gloucester's ambitions:

'Henry and his sons are gone; thou, Clarence, art next;
And one by one I will dispatch the rest,
Counting myself but bad till I be best.'

The True Tragedy..., Act 5 Scene 6, lines 90–92

Before Shakespeare completed his account of the lives of Henry VI, Edward IV and Richard III, he worked on *Titus Andronicus*. Written around 1591 or a little earlier, when there was a vogue for gory tales of revenge in which horror piles on horror, *Titus* translates Latin models of this kind into a thoroughly English idiom. Shakespeare's main model was the Roman dramatist Seneca, many of whose tragedies were being translated at this time. They are as full of highly theatrical revenge killings as any Hollywood gangster film, as terrifying as any horror movie. If on the page the action seems ludicrous, in performance audiences can still be moved to terror and pity. The language is formal and has the effect of distancing the events from the onlooker. We watch Tamora, Queen of the Goths, avenge her son's death by enabling her other sons, Demetrius and Chiron, to rape her captor Titus's daughter, Lavinia, then cut off her hands and pull out her tongue to prevent her from telling who did it. We watch as Titus is tricked into cutting off his hand in order, as he thinks, to save his own sons' lives. We watch Titus and his brother Marcus kill the rapists, cook them and serve them up in a pie to be eaten by their mother. We watch Titus kill Lavinia to remove her shame and then kill Tamora herself. We watch Tamora's husband kill Titus and then be killed by Titus's last remaining son, Lucius. Just as in Ancient Greek tragedy the chorus[†] wore masks with wide open eyes so that they could not turn away from the terrifying scenes they were called on to witness, so Shakespeare's formal language has the effect of distancing the events from us but keeping us openeyed to wonder at the blood being spilt before us and to pity the waste of so much life.

In early 1592 Shakespeare returned to English history with a play now generally referred to as *Henry VI Part 1* in which the events leading up to the struggles of *The Contention...* and *The True Tragedy* (i.e.

Henry VI Parts 2 and 3) are recounted. Many scholars think Shakespeare was not solely responsible for the play but collaborated with at least two other authors (a very common practice in the Elizabethan theatre).

Henry VI Part 1 shows how the unity of England fell apart after the death of King Henry V. All the way through the play, Shakespeare and his collaborators use dramatic techniques to pull historical events widely spread in time into a single scene. The play opens, for example, with nobles bickering at King Henry's funeral while messengers arrive to tell of the loss of those lands in France that the late king had won back for England, losses which in fact took place over several years. It goes on to tell of the growth of the two factions of the white rose (York) and the red rose (Lancaster), symbolized by a scene (Act 2 Scene 4, probably one of those written by Shakespeare) in a garden where the opposed forces choose roses to advertise their allegiance and the Earl of Warwick draws back the veil of history:

'this brawl today,
Grown to this faction in the Temple garden,
Shall send, between the red rose and the white,
A thousand souls to death and deadly night'
Henry VI Part 1, Act 2 Scene 4, lines 124–127

The play ends with wars in France. The French are portrayed as treacherous and their hero, Joan of Arc, as a witch. But the wars allow a hero to emerge in Lord Talbot before he and his son are betrayed by the squabbling between the Yorkists and Lancastrians and, deprived of troops to support them, they die valiantly but uselessly.

If *Henry VI Part 1* establishes the in-fighting which was to lead to civil war, *Richard III*, written probably a few months later towards the end of 1592, brings it all to a bloody conclusion.

In the earlier plays about Henry VI and the Wars of the Roses, Shakespeare had begun to play with history to create dramatic effects. In this play he is even less concerned to let history stand in the way of a good story. The sources he used were themselves highly biased accounts written by supporters of Henry VII and the Tudors who had defeated Richard. Shakespeare was not to know this, but he played with even the information and the timescales that he had in order to focus all our attention on Richard's climb to the throne by a process of lying, cheating, manipulating and murdering his opponents and his friends. And yet, like so many dramatic portraits of evil, this Richard is mesmerizing – he plays with the other characters and with the audience like a snake with a rabbit. He is energetic and witty, always a step ahead of the rest, until his conscience catches up with him and he falls to what Shakespeare invites us to see as the force of good – Henry Richmond who becomes Henry VII, Queen Elizabeth's grandfather.

Although it may not be accurate history, in Richard, Shakespeare created his first full-blooded villain to stand alongside the overreaching characters of Christopher Marlowe. Marlowe's Jew of Malta, named Barabas, and Shakespeare's King Richard both proclaim themselves as followers of the Italian analyser of political power games, Niccoló Machiavelli. Modern scholarship has shown that Machiavelli's work is a complex and not necessarily approving picture of how rulers can gain power and stay in control, but in the English popular imagination at the end of the 16th century he was a by-word for evil. When in *The True Tragedy...* Shakespeare has Richard say that he will 'set the murderous Machiavel to school' (Act 3 Scene 2), he makes it clear that this man will stop at nothing to gain power, and will cheat and murder his way to the throne.

These early plays lay out a number of themes which Shakespeare was to develop throughout his working life. In the comedies *The Two Gentlemen of Verona* and *The Taming of the Shrew* he explores ideas of friendship, love and marriage, showing how relationships shift and change when under pressure. He is also experimenting with ways of showing the complexity of human beings. Few of his characters, even in these early plays, are simple or act from unmixed motives. As Shakespeare's skill develops through the exploration of politics and history – and he seems effectively to have invented the history play form – so the gap between appearance and reality widens. The naive disguise of characters such as Julia in *Two Gentlemen* becomes the dissembling of politicians such as the Duke of Somerset in *The True Tragedy...* or the revengers Tamora and Titus Andronicus, and reaches a climax in Richard III's lethal manoeuvrings. Again, the language of the plays becomes at once simpler, more direct, but at the same time carries richer and more telling ambiguity. In a world where no one ever quite means what they say, and actions are two-edged swords, the pretence of the playhouse has become the ideal medium for examining human life.

THE PLAYHOUSES

Plays need playing places. The requirements of audibility and visibility imply either a raised stage or banked-up seating (as in Ancient Greek and Roman theatres and the *plen-an-gwarries* [playing places] in Cornwall), and a way of focusing the player's voice while blocking out unnecessary noise. The medieval plays associated with Corpus Christi[†] were performed either on and around carts or on specially erected stages. For other occasions wooden stages, which were called scaffolds, might be erected inside churches, market halls, the great halls of houses, university colleges and schools, or simply in the open air. Such stages were temporary affairs. For example, between 1546 and about 1638, Queens' College, Cambridge, had a scaffold made up of 500 pieces of timber, erected once a year in the hall and kept in storage the rest of the time. The tradition that inns were used for performances by touring companies, in London or around the country, maybe required similar temporary arrangements – clearing out a room or erecting a scaffold in the courtyard if it was big enough.

The first specially built public playhouse opened in Great Yarmouth in about 1538, but the first in London was the Red Lion, built in 1567 by a grocer, John Brayne. The name of this playhouse has led people to think it was an inn, but this is not the case. Legal documents have recently come to light which show that it was essentially designed and built from scratch by Brayne in the courtyard of a farmhouse situated just outside the Aldgate on what is now Whitechapel High Street. We know little more about the Red Lion but are on firmer ground with the

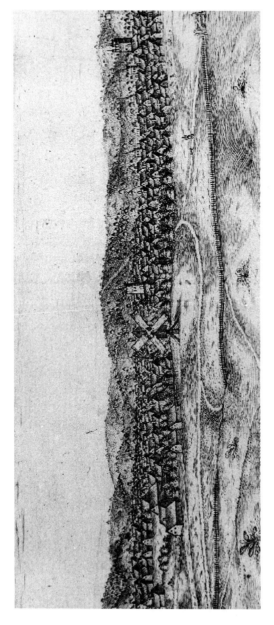

Part of an engraving of London, viewed from the north about 1597. The building with the flag may be The Theatre, built by James Burbage in 1576. The engraving is now in the Utrecht University Library, Holland.

playhouse built by Brayne's brother-in-law, James Burbage – leading light in Leicester's Men and father of Richard Burbage, Shakespeare's famous future fellow player.

Burbage's playhouse was called The Theatre and was built in 1576 on a site west of what is now Shoreditch High Street and north of Holywell Lane. A year later another playhouse, The Curtain, was built, probably by Henry Lanman, on the other side of Holywell Lane.

The building of The Theatre was the result of the new situation for companies such as Leicester's Men. Their licence allowed them to perform daily, if not in the city, then in its Liberties[†] – places like Shoreditch just outside the city walls. Temporary arrangements in other buildings hardly allowed such regular arrangements to be made. But there are other implications:

1. The companies were, with the exception of the Queen's Men, essentially business ventures. We know that in 1599 it cost one penny to stand for a play at The Curtain, another penny to have a seat and a further penny for a seat with a cushion and a good view. As popular entertainers, players could earn good money and, as always in such cases, the entrepreneurs who laid out the initial capital and took the financial risks could make a fortune. We will see that this is what happened as the playhouses developed.

2. Playhouses were used by more than one company. The Theatre may have been a home for Leicester's Men but before it was demolished in 1598 (and its timbers used to build the first Globe Theatre) at least six other companies played there, including Shakespeare's companies, Lord Strange's Men and the

Lord Chamberlain's Men. It is likely that the early plays of Shakespeare and those of Christopher Marlowe, had their first London performances on the stage of The Theatre.

3. The contrast between The Theatre and The Curtain shows that the London theatre scene in Shakespeare's time was very varied. The Theatre probably attracted a more affluent, serious playgoer than The Curtain which became famous for its unruly audiences, bawdy shows and crowd-pleasing spectacles.

4. The Theatre and The Curtain (like the Red Lion and most other later London playhouses) were situated just outside the city walls. As we have already seen, there was a constant tension between the city authorities and the playing companies who were looked on with some suspicion as spreaders of plague[†], vice, crime, immorality and sedition. Pleasures were on offer in the Liberties, and playhouses jostled with bear-baiting or bull-baiting and brothels to attract customers. We can be sure that playhouse owners were earning money from these other entertainments, too.

At the end of Chapter 3 we asked 'Are plays controlled expressions of religious or political power, or are they anarchic explosions – carnivals of the human spirit?' As the playing companies and their playing places developed during the 16th century, this question became more acute. The companies were controlled by royal licence and linked to noble patrons[†]. They were expected to be available to perform at court or at the houses of their patrons to add to the magnificent display which established power in the land. But at the same time the playhouses were in the Liberties, on the margins of the city. In that sense players were both at the centre and on the margins of society. But the energy of their work brought the anarchy to the centre: it is not coincidental that they were called to court to perform at the times of the Lord of Misrule[†] and Carnival – after Christmas and before the beginning of Lent.

In this sense the Liberties were the natural home of the players. Into those marginal places, north of the city walls and south of the river, Elizabethan society banished all its fears: death – here were the hospitals, places of execution and cemeteries; sex – the brothels were here; and the animal instincts and pleasures – bull- and bear-baiting, cock-fighting. And here too were the players, whose stories disturb, overturn and lay bare the hidden motives of men and women. In the playhouses of the Liberties these fears could be addressed and if not tamed, then controlled, and allowed back in through the city gates. In Shakespeare's early plays this ambivalence of order and chaos is already being held up to the light.

6
PLAGUE, POEMS AND PATRONS

London stank. Its rivers were thick with filth and its rapidly growing population walked along streets made slippery by sewage. Wherever two or three families were gathered together there was likely to be a dunghill. Vegetable plots were watered from drainage ditches. Alive with rats, fleas and lice, the houses were breeding grounds of disease and in the overcrowded streets it spread like wildfire. The people lived in fear of plague[†].

Bubonic plague had been a constant threat in England since 1348–50, the years of the Black Death which wiped out about 25 per cent of the population of Europe (perhaps 40 million people). During the 16th and 17th centuries hardly a year went by without an outbreak in London and elsewhere in the country. There was a severe outbreak in Stratford in 1564, the year Shakespeare was born.

Bubonic plague was the most feared of all epidemic diseases. It is spread by the bite of parasitic insects that normally live on rats. The heat of summer and the filthy conditions of the towns inevitably led to outbreaks of the disease as rats and their parasites bred uncontrollably. Anyone infected would develop a headache and a general sense of tiredness, and soon they would begin to vomit and their joints ache. Within hours the groin and the areas under the arm or on the side of the neck began to swell and the patient started to run a temperature. The disease was a fast but painful killer: the swellings (called buboes, hence bubonic plague) increased to the size of a chicken's egg, the pulse began to race and breathing became harder until, within about four days, the patient turned purple as their lungs failed, and death put an end to their intense suffering. Not knowing the cause of plague, no proper measures could be taken to effect a cure, although town and city authorities tried their best by banning gatherings that might spread the infection (including performances at playhouses), and those who could got out of the cities, heavy with the stench of death and decay, and into the country – though often taking the infection with them.

In June 1592, with the plague threatening once more, the London authorities, already alarmed by a riot of apprentices[†] a few days earlier, proclaimed that no plays could be performed, even in the Liberties[†], because the crowds gathering there might spread the disease. This might have been an excuse to reduce the threat of disturbance – London was suffering the effects of economic failure and famine – but it certainly prevented the players from earning a living. The prohibition was reaffirmed in January 1593 and the playhouses remained closed for the rest of that year.

We know that players went out on the road again, including a group from Lord Strange's Men who toured during the summer of 1593, probably taking some of Shakespeare's plays with them. It is possible that Shakespeare joined them but his name does not appear on the licence permitting the company to play as the Earl of Pembroke's Men, and the bankruptcy of the rest of the company – forced to sell personal effects and their stock of plays that same autumn – does not seem to have affected Shakespeare. In 1592 he was probably living in a northern area of the city badly hit by plague. Maybe he took this opportunity to return home to Stratford and explore other writing options.

Doctor Samuel Johnson, compiling his famous *Dictionary of the English Language*, which was published in 1755, defined a person who makes dictionaries as 'a harmless drudge'. He could also have been describing most playwrights of Shakespeare's, and most other, times. There was money to be made in the playhouses but it went to the owner, the players, even the provider of food and drink to the audience, rather than to the writer. This is not altogether unfair. After all, the idea of a play text as a piece of literature – something to be read like a novel or a poem – is very modern. If plays were printed at all during Shakespeare's lifetime, that was likely to mean they had reached the end of their useful life for a company, or had been given to a printer against their wishes. Like the score of a piece of music, a play text is only properly in existence when it is being performed. Real meaning emerges only in the layers of interaction between the actors, and between actors and audience. The writer's role is significant – and Shakespeare's contribution to the raised status of playwrights is crucial – but only as a partner. Playwrights and actors know just how much the text performed on the opening night is the product of collaboration during its preparation, and it may well change again with the experience of performance. We have every reason to suppose that it was no different for Shakespeare.

HENRY WRIOTHESLEY, EARL OF SOUTHAMPTON

To be noticed, even to earn a living, a writer had to find someone who would support, protect, and, with luck, pay him. The best way, then as now, was to appeal to vanity, to flatter a potential patron[†] by dedicating a work of art to him which, like gold-dust sticking to his fingers, would make the rich man shine all the brighter.

The two poems Shakespeare wrote, and had printed, between the autumn of 1592 and May 1594 were dedicated to Henry Wriothesley, Earl of Southampton, at that time a boy of 18. Southampton was a friend of the Earl of Essex, a great favourite of the queen. They shared a desire to be brave and glorious courtiers and soldiers after the manner of one of the most famous men of the time, Sir Philip Sidney, who had died of wounds sustained in fighting in the Low Countries (Netherlands) in 1586. But there were few foreign wars to fight and their ambitions were frustrated by the older noblemen who were the queen's advisers. Full of ambition to glitter like the princes at the European courts, they were limited instead to petty intrigues and the tedium of life in the royal palaces.

VENUS AND ADONIS

There is no evidence that Shakespeare knew Southampton before he dedicated *Venus and Adonis* to him in February 1593. The letter at the start of the poem could simply be a few well-turned phrases aimed at attracting his attention. But within the dedication an interesting phrase stands out. Shakespeare refers to the book as 'the first heir of my invention'. Presumably it was his first printed work, but it also perhaps indicates how little Shakespeare either rated or wanted to draw attention to the plays for which he was becoming well-known. Advertising yourself as a playwright or player was not necessarily the right way to commend yourself to a nobleman.

Among the books that a grammar school[†] boy would have read were the *Metamorphoses* of Ovid, a Latin author. The stories which Ovid tells concern mysterious and miraculous changes, and with their constant interchange between appearance and reality would be likely to have fascinated Shakespeare. The story of Venus and Adonis takes up 75 lines of Book 10. Shakespeare expands it to 1194 lines made up of six-line verses. In doing so, he changes the poem with disturbing effect. In Ovid, the handsome youth Adonis returns the love of the goddess Venus. In Shakespeare, Adonis tries to avoid her:

> 'She red and hot as coals of glowing fire;
> He red for shame, but frosty in desire.'
>
> *Venus and Adonis, lines 35–36*

These lines already make clear the structure of the rhetoric[†] in the verse. Both Venus and Adonis are 'red', but she for lust, he for shame. The rhyming couplets regularly create such effects which balance and draw a contrast at the same time. It gives the effect of drawing Venus and Adonis together while keeping them separate. It is one of Shakespeare's most characteristic rhetorical devices, found in plays as well as poems.

As the poem develops, Shakespeare draws away from his model. Venus and Adonis become complex characters and their interplay increasingly realistic. Adonis sets off on a fatal hunt to try to get away from Venus. She waits anxiously for news, fears the worst, finds his body, and laments his death:

'Alas, poor world, what treasure hast thou lost,
What face remains alive that's worth the viewing?
Whose tongue is music now? What canst thou boast
Of things long since, or anything ensuing?
    The flowers are sweet, their colours fresh and trim;
    But true sweet beauty lived and died with him.'

Venus and Adonis, lines 1075–1080

The lovers are flesh and blood, making the erotic charge of the poem all the greater. And when it comes to the transformation at the end of the poem, this realism finally pays off. In Ovid, the dead Adonis is changed into a flower, an anemone; in Shakespeare one real thing – a dead boy – is replaced by another – the flower:

'By this, the boy that by her side lay killed
Was melted like a vapour from her sight,
And in his blood that on the ground lay spilled
A purple flower sprang up, chequered with white,
    Resembling well his pale cheeks, and the blood
    Which in round drops upon their whiteness stood.'

Venus and Adonis, 1165–1170

THE RAPE OF LUCRECE

Fourteen months later, in May 1594, and with the playhouses re-opening, a second poem, *The Rape of Lucrece*, was dedicated to Southampton. The letter at the beginning of the book is more relaxed, even more friendly. This time it speaks of 'the warrant I have of your honourable disposition' – some positive response, or even a payment of money? – and how 'my duty... is bound to your lordship'. Some sort of relationship appears to have opened up.

The Rape of Lucrece is also based on Ovid, but is a tragic story of lust and rape, the exact reverse of *Venus and Adonis*. In the earlier poem, the woman tried to seduce the man, here the man rapes the woman. Adonis dies hunting a boar, Lucrece kills herself. The verses have seven lines and the rhetorical effect is darker.

In *The Rape of Lucrece* Shakespeare explored worlds like those of the great tragedies[†] written some years later. Tarquin is a portrait of vicious lust:

> 'Into the chamber wickedly he stalks,
> And gazeth on her yet-unstainèd bed.
> The curtains being close, about he walks,
> Rolling his greedy eye-balls in his head.'
>
> *The Rape of Lucrece*, lines 365–370

Lucrece reveals her feelings through soliloquies (a speech when one actor alone expresses thoughts and feelings to the audience), much as Hamlet or Macbeth or King Lear will do:

> 'Where now I have no one to blush with me,
> To cross their arms and hang their heads with mine,
> To mask their brows and hide their infamy,
> But I alone, alone must sit and pine,
> Seasoning the earth with showers of silver brine,
>   Mingling my talk with tears, my grief with groans,
>   Poor wasting monuments of lasting moans.'
>
> *The Rape of Lucrece*, lines 792–798

LOVE'S LABOUR'S LOST

One aspect of Elizabethan poetry which modern readers can find particularly difficult is its love of elegant and complicated word-play. As well as the rhetorical techniques we have seen in *Venus and Adonis*, writers

81

and readers delighted in puns, hidden messages, allusions to events, authors, people. It is as if the poems were complex and witty coded messages depending on secret knowledge for full understanding. At about the same time that he was writing the two poems, Shakespeare was also working on a new play, *Love's Labour's Lost*. Unusually for him, the plot was his own invention (Shakespeare generally borrowed basic stories from elsewhere which he then twisted and developed to give new insights). It concerns the King of Navarre and his three friends who have decided to live in isolation from women and undertake academic study. Almost at once the Princess of France and three of her ladies arrive on a diplomatic mission. Predictably the men fall in love and there is much comic confusion as they try to hide the fact from each other. The confusions grow as the men, disguised as Russians, come to entertain the women who in the meantime, to make fun of the men, have swapped identities. The language of these characters is a dazzling display of verbal wit very like the poetry Shakespeare was in the process of dedicating to the Earl of Southampton, but its limitations as an expression of human life (and so the limitations of human life which can only be lived through witty display) are shown in a number of ways. First, the comic characters' attempts to use similar wit fall flat (with hilarious results). Second, Costard the clown and his girlfriend Jacquenetta are a couple who need no words as a substitute for love. And third, near the end of the play a messenger, Mercadé, arrives with bad news.

It is this moment which shows most clearly the difference between poetry and a play. Mercadé's entrance from the 'real' world of pain and death reminds characters and audience alike of the limitations of wit. The impact depends on his physical presence, a silent figure among the chattering lovers and wordy fools. His language is simple and direct, needing no display to give its message, which can, indeed, hardly be spoken:

Mercadé: God save you, madam.
Princess: Welcome, Mercadé,
                 But that thou interrupt's our merriment.
Mercadé: I am sorry, madam, for the news I bring
                 Is heavy in my tongue. The King your father -
Princess: Dead, for my life.
Mercadé: Even so. My tale is told.
Biron: Worthies, away. The scene begins to cloud.

Love's Labour's Lost, Act 5 Scene 2, lines 709–715

THE LONDON BOOK TRADE

The book you are now reading comes to you through five basic steps. First, the writer produces a text – a manuscript. Second, a publisher accepts the text and decides to make it more widely available. Third, a printer turns the text into many identical copies. Fourth, a bookseller obtains copies from the publisher and puts them on sale. And finally, potential readers buy the book. This modern process is essentially no different from that by which Shakespeare's poems and some of his early plays were made available to readers in Elizabethan England.

The centre of the London book trade at that time was the streets around old St Paul's Cathedral. Here writers would come to try to find someone interested in publishing their book. Once that was done the text

83

still had to be approved for publication by an officer of the church, and licensed by the Guild of Stationers, who controlled book production. The licence was given only when it was agreed that the publication of a book would not affect the rights of anyone else. Finally the book was entered on the Register of the Guild which allowed a printer to go ahead and print it.

The streets around St Paul's were full of booksellers' stalls and printers' workshops, identified by a sign hanging outside (street numbers were an 18th-century invention). *Venus and Adonis* was available at the shop displaying 'the signe of the Angel' and at John Harrison's shop beneath 'the sign of the White Greyhound', for example. Some bookshops probably specialized in the books they sold, others took what they thought would sell, but just as any printer might be approached to produce a book, so any bookseller could obtain copies for their shop. On 12 June 1593, a man named Richard Stonely was looking around the bookshops. He stopped at John Harrison's and bought 'the Venus & Adhonay pr Shakspear' ('the *Venus and Adonis* by Shakespeare' – spelling was a notoriously slippery art in Shakespeare's time), probably for sixpence.

Venus and Adonis and *The Rape of Lucrece* were printed by John Field, a man three years older than Shakespeare and also from Stratford. The two would have been at school together before Field was sent to London to be apprenticed into the printing trade. When Shakespeare looked for someone to produce his first printed books, we must assume he turned to an old friend who had begun to specialize in printing high-quality texts. For his first publications, Shakespeare was determined to have the best.

7
ENTERTAINERS AND ENTREPRENEURS

Theatre is an expensive business. The great cycles of mystery plays† cost a great deal to perform, and by the early 16th century demands for better staging and better actors were making them, for most towns, a costly luxury. The pageants†, tournaments and other entertainments by which kings and noblemen reinforced their power were also hugely expensive. The economics of the 16th century placed ready money into the hands of a larger group of tradesmen, farmers, merchants and the professions and, although the legal status of players remained as servants of the aristocracy, in reality from at least the 1580s playing companies were business concerns. Of course this met the needs of the courtiers too: so long as they could call on the services of the players from time to time for their own entertainments, the companies could be self-supporting.

The playing companies were in the business of making money, and the profits could be substantial. There were essentially two ways of making money from playhouses. One was to own one of them, or have sole rights of some kind within them. So James Burbage made his money from The Theatre and Henry Lanman from The Curtain while, from 1587, Philip Henslowe held the lease of The Rose, a playhouse built south of the River Thames in the Liberty† of the Clink. Henslowe's partner, John Cholmley, took over a cottage near The Rose to provide refreshments for playgoers, and he had sole rights to provide food and drink on the site.

The other way to make money was to manage or be a sharer† in a playing company, which could include owning the plays that were performed. James Burbage and Philip Henslowe were rival managers, on each side of the river. In May 1591 Burbage was in dispute with his players (the combined Lord Strange's and Admiral's Men) at The Theatre. They accused him of keeping back some of their share of takings. Some of the players, led by the star Edward Alleyn, walked out and went across the river to form the core of Henslowe's company at The Rose. They would have taken some of their repertoire of plays with them – perhaps Alleyn owned them – but, with the exception of *Titus Andronicus*, none of them appears to have been by Shakespeare. It is possible that Richard Burbage, James's son, owned the rest of Shapespeare's plays at this time. Richard was probably linked with the ill-fated Pembroke's Men whose touring life ended disastrously in 1593, after which some, at least, of the plays were printed to raise money.

The financial arrangements at The Rose give a good picture of how the income was shared out. Henslowe received money from Cholmley four times a year as part of the agreement for the sale of refreshments. In turn, Cholmley kept the profits from the 'breade and drinke'. Henslowe had paid for the construction of the theatre and provided money for the costumes and other items for the performance. (He kept meticulous account books which give us much of our information about playhouse performances at the time.) Henslowe and Cholmley shared the responsibility for finding players and they both agreed to be present at performances, to keep an eye on the takings. Henslowe and Cholmley shared on a fifty-fifty basis half the money taken from the sale of gallery seats. The other half of the gallery takings, and all the income from those standing in the yard in front of the stage, went to the actors to be divided up between them.

A year after he arrived at The Rose, in 1592, Alleyn married Henslowe's step-daughter, Joan Woodward, and they began to take a greater part in running the family firm. After Alleyn's arrival Philip Henslowe seems to have concentrated less on the playhouse and more on his other lucrative interests – bull- and bear-baiting and brothels. Alleyn retired from the stage in about 1597 (though had a brief return shortly after 1600 and played the part of Genius for King James's procession into London in March 1604). He became wealthy enough to found a school and hospital south-east of London (now Dulwich College) in 1613 before he died in 1626.

In 1594 a group of actors, probably including many of those who had stayed with James Burbage at The Theatre, formed themselves into a new company and gained the patronage[†] of Lord Hunsdon, who was shortly to become Lord Chamberlain[†]. The Queen's Men had finally disintegrated in 1594, and a certain amount of re-organization of the players seems to have taken place that summer. The main companies were the Admiral's Men and the Lord Chamberlain's Men. The Admiral's Men included Edward Alleyn, and probably his brother John, George Attewell, James Tunstall, Thomas Downton, Richard Jones, the clown John Singer, Thomas Towne, Martin Slater and Edward Juby. The Lord Chamberlain's Men included Thomas Pope, George Bryan and the clown Will Kemp (who had all been with Leicester's Men and had performed at Elsinore in Denmark, the setting for *Hamlet*, in 1586), Augustine Phillips, John Heminges, Richard Cowley, John Sincler, William Sly, John Duke, Robert Gough, and Richard Burbage, with possibly Nicholas Tooley, Henry Condell, Alexander Cooke and Christopher Beeston. William Shakespeare was almost certainly a member of this company too. During June 1594 both companies were performing at The Rose but after that the Chamberlain's Men went back over the river to The Theatre, where they stayed until its closure in 1598.

Players who became sharers[†] in their company (and not all of them did – some were simply employees, paid weekly, while others were apprentices[†] of the more experienced men) were able to make a good deal of money. Thomas Pope, for instance, was described as a 'gentleman' – implying status and wealth – when he died in 1604. By 1619 Henry Condell was described as 'of great living, wealth and power' and by 1625 was living in a country house in Fulham, while a clown called Thomas Sackville moved to Germany where he invested in a silk business and died a rich man. Player-sharers who died poor, like Will Kemp, probably had only themselves to blame.

It is important to remember that there were no women in the playing companies in Shakespeare's time. All women's parts were played by boys or by men who specialized in female roles.

When the Lord Chamberlain's Men were formed, William Shakespeare was probably living in St Helen's parish in the north of the city (the area now east of Bishopsgate and bounded by Camomile Street and Crosby Square). Certainly he owned property there in

1596 because he was assessed for tax purposes. (He failed to pay the full amount and was named as a defaulter a year later.)

In October 1594 the Lord Chamberlain asked the city authorities to allow his company to use the Cross Keys Inn in Gracechurch Street (the southbound continuation of Bishopsgate) for winter performances, and possibly for rehearsal purposes. They played at court on 26 December and then, two days later, in the Hall of Gray's Inn, one of the centres of London's legal profession, presented another play: *The Comedy of Errors* by William Shakespeare.

THE COMEDY OF ERRORS

For his first new work after the re-opening of the playhouses, Shakespeare returned to the Latin plays he would have read at school. Plautus's *Menaechmi* was about a man searching for his twin brother who is thrown into confusion when everyone he meets mistakes him for that brother. We know that it was performed by the boys of St Paul's School in 1527 and no doubt was a regular entertainment in schools and universities. *The Comedy of Errors* is as tightly constructed as any of its Latin models, but Shakespeare doubles the potential for confusion by having two pairs of twins. He also makes the distinctively Shakespearean move of setting the play within a framework of death. Old Egeon, a merchant, searching for his sons parted at birth, has arrived at Ephesus from Syracuse despite a decree that any Syracusans found in the town will be executed. He is arrested and given a day to find someone to pay a ransom. Unknown to him, his son Antipholus (of Syracuse) has also arrived with his servant Dromio (of Syracuse). The confusions begin as both of them are mistaken for their twin brothers, also called Antipholus and Dromio, who live in Ephesus.

The serious frame sets up dramatic possibilities. The unravelling of the confusion becomes, literally, a matter of life and death. It also enables Shakespeare to begin to explore ideas about being a twin, which continued to fascinate him. We have seen that he was the father of twins, Judith and Hamnet, born in 1585 (Hamnet was to die, aged 11, in August 1596), and he seems to have gained a deep understanding of what it means to be a twin, and the pain of separation. On his own near the beginning of the play, Antipholus of Syracuse says:

> 'He that commends me to mine own content
> Commends me to the thing I cannot get.
> I to the world am like a drop of water
> That in the ocean seeks another drop...'
>
> *The Comedy of Errors*, Act 1 Scene 2, lines 33–36

After all the confusions have been cleared up and mistakes put right, after the brothers have found one another and Egeon has found not only his sons but also his long lost wife who has become abbess of a nunnery in Ephesus, the servant Dromio of Ephesus ends the play:

> 'We came into the world like brother and brother,
> And now let's go hand in hand, not one before another.'
>
> *The Comedy of Errors*, Act 5 Scene 1, lines 429–430

Ephesus is a place of magic – famous in ancient times for witchcraft and sorcery – and this too is an early indication of a theme that will recur throughout Shakespeare's later plays. In the 'real' world of pain and death and confusion we need to step into another place, where appearance and reality become confused, before we can discover the truth about ourselves.

A MIDSUMMER NIGHT'S DREAM

Over ten years later the tragic King Lear had to go out into a stormy wilderness before he began to understand himself, but Shakespeare's own next place of mystery was a very English wood 'outside Athens'.

A Midsummer Night's Dream was probably written in 1594 or 1595. There is no evidence to support the tradition that it was written as part of a wedding celebration, although one of its interlocking concerns is how marriage can bring differences together. *A Dream* is constructed from a whole range of sources and ideas, including transformations to be found in Ovid's *Metamorphoses*. It brings together, too, so many of the ideas we have seen Shakespeare exploring up to now: appearance and reality, separation and discovery, love and sex, the hidden instincts and passions and the outward presentation of ourselves, the natural and the supernatural.

Once more the framing technique is used. The play starts and finishes in Duke Theseus's palace in Athens. It opens as he is preparing to marry Hippolyta, Queen of the Amazons. There is tension in the air. As the Duke reminds Hippolyta:

'...I wooed thee with my sword,
And won thy love doing thee injuries.
But I will wed thee in another key –

With pomp, with triumph, and with revelling.'
A Midsummer Night's Dream, Act I Scene I, lines 16–19

Other tensions crowd in immediately: Hermia, betrothed to Demetrius, is in love with Lysander. Demetrius loves Hermia but used to love Helena, who is still in love with him. Hermia and Lysander decide to run away through the forest to be married. Helena, hoping to get back into Demetrius's favour, tells him what the lovers are doing. Thus love becomes a source of confusion and a battleground.

Just as in *Love's Labour's Lost* and *The Two Gentlemen of Verona*, the romance is set against the antics of stock comic characters, so here the wood is filled not only with fleeing and pursuing lovers but also with a bunch of workmen rehearsing a play to be performed at the Duke's wedding. Peter Quince and his company are to play *The Most Lamentable Comedy and Most Cruel Death of Pyramus and Thisbe*, another story from Ovid. Again we are thrust into confusion: is it a tragedy[†] or a comedy? A boy will play a girl (they always did in Shakespeare's theatre – here it is brought into the open and its confusions advertised). A lion will roar 'as gentle as any sucking dove'.

In rapid time three layers have been introduced; now comes a fourth. The wood is home to the king and queen of the fairies, Oberon and Titania, and they are in the middle of a bitter quarrel. Once more tension is overcoming love, but now the effect is much greater – the quarrels of the fairies have affected the natural world:

'The spring, the summer,
The chiding autumn, angry winter change

Their wonted liveries, and the mazèd world
By their increase knows not which is which;
And this same progeny of evils comes
From our debate, from our dissension.
We are their parents and original.'

A Midsummer Night's Dream, Act 2 Scene 1, lines 111–117

The lovers, the workmen and the fairies are all in the wood together and the tensions and confusions increase. So do the transformations. Oberon sends his servant Puck for a flower, the juice of which will make anyone into whose eye it is squeezed love the first thing they see. With this flower they try to put the lovers' quarrel to rights but get it wrong and Lysander and Demetrius both transfer their love to Helena! Now Oberon plays a cruel trick on Titania: squeezing the juice into her eyes he then transforms Bottom the weaver, one of the would-be actors, into an ass, and makes sure Titania will see him when she wakes. As soon as she sees him she is full of desire and they go off to make love. Love and desire have disintegrated everywhere into fear and lust.

Eventually Oberon and Puck put things back as they should be: Lysander loves Hermia, Demetrius Helena, Titania and Oberon are reunited and Bottom is changed back into a human being. There have been dreams, but none more amazing than Bottom's:

'I have had a most rare vision. I have had a dream past the
wit of man to say what dream it was. Methought I was -
there is no man can tell what... It shall be called 'Bottom's
Dream' because it hath no bottom, and... I shall sing
it at her death.'

A Midsummer Night's Dream, Act 4 Scene 1, lines 202–206

Again, as the magic fades, Shakespearean ideas crowd together. The play has been full of complex and witty verse but as the dream ends we are left with simple, direct language. In the face of the deepest truth, no words are adequate.

The earlier comic effect of mixing romance and knock-about farce† is more integrated in this play. The multi-layered world of fairies, kings, lovers and clowns who become animals is shown as a single reality. Perhaps the whole play grows out of the marital and sexual anxieties of Theseus and Hippolyta. To win her he must woo her and bed her, showing her the layers of desire that true love requires.

A Midsummer Night's Dream is a disturbing and wonderful play of the imagination. There are transformations; people, their feelings and their understanding change. But like Adonis and the anemone at the end of *Venus and Adonis*, one thing does not turn into another. Perhaps Shakespeare's great insight here is that the creative imagination works with resemblances: things stay as they are – boys and flowers, weavers and asses, Amazon Queens and Fairy Queens – but they gain new meaning from their likeness to each other. Plays are no different. A player does not become a character – Puck or Bottom or Oberon – rather, the player and character are there together, inhabiting the same time and space. One of the functions of the performance of *Pyramus and Thisbe* is that it illuminates the themes we have seen in the rest of the play. Bottom is transformed again, this time by playing the lover Pyramus who loses Thisbe – but he remains Bottom the weaver who has lost the Queen of the Fairies.

Even before this final knockabout story of love and separation, Duke Theseus and Hippolyta begin to understand:

Theseus: Such tricks hath strong imagination
That if it would but apprehend some joy
It comprehends some bringer of that joy;
Or in the night, imagining some fear,
How easy is a bush supposed a bear!

Hippolyta: But all the story of the night told over,
And all their minds transfigured so together,
More witnesseth than fancy's images,
And grows to something of great constancy;
But howsoever, strange and admirable.

A Midsummer Night's Dream, Act 5 Scene 1, lines 18–27

A Midsummer Night's Dream without bottom! In its final most typically Shakespearean twist the play remains open-ended. The newly-weds go to bed and the fairies have blessed the house. Then comes Puck, apologizing, and saying that if anyone is offended they should see it as 'just a dream'. But like any dream it has no easy interpretation; we cannot say it is about this, or that. Once more Shakespeare invites us in to the power of a play: its meaning is uncertain and our own thoughts and feelings, hopes and fears make an important contribution too. In his last lines Puck offers his hands to the audience, inviting us all to join in the circle of imagination and understanding:

'Give me your hands, if we be friends,
And Robin shall restore amends.'

A Midsummer Night's Dream, Epilogue, lines 15–16

THE MERCHANT OF VENICE

During the later 1590s, Shakespeare wrote or contributed to at least 12 plays for his company. The tradition of love stories begun with *The Two Gentlemen of Verona* was developed in *Romeo and Juliet* and *Much Ado About Nothing* and turned into something more complex in *The Merchant of Venice*.

By 1596 or 1597 when *The Merchant of Venice* was probably written, William Shakespeare was an experienced man of the theatre who was increasingly able to put together plays with many layers of plot and meaning. On the surface *The Merchant of Venice* seems a simple story of a wicked Jew trying to trick and kill Christians and being outsmarted. But it is full of insight into human nature: it deals with serious matters (though it can raise many smiles as well), and darkness and pain are never far away. It has been criticized for being anti-Semitic – for using prejudice against Jews – to comic effect, but this is too simple. The more closely we examine the play the more ambiguous it becomes.

First of all, it is about a merchant. In 1598 it was referred to as '*The Merchant of Venice* or otherwise called *The Jew of Venice*'; we immediately have an uncertainty. Is the central character Antonio, the Christian merchant, or the Jew, Shylock? Whichever, they are both concerned with trade: the play is about love and friendship, but these are inextricably linked with making deals and taking chances, with honesty and trust. In *The Taming of the Shrew*, Shakespeare had already shown that marriage proposals can be conducted like trade deals, and in a world where marriages were often basically business deals his audience would understand just what was going on.

The play is about a merchant and a money-lender. Antonio and Shylock each has something the other wants: the Christian wants the Jew's money to finance business arrangements; Shylock wants the respect and social standing which as a Jew he cannot have. It is worth remembering that Shakespeare grew up in the world of trade and never really wholly left it behind. His father was a merchant and money-lender, and almost certainly William was, too. His father was nearly imprisoned for debt. The world of this play was one Shakespeare knew inside out.

Second, *The Merchant of Venice* is about justice. Antonio has borrowed money to finance his friend Bassanio's attempt to marry Portia, a rich heiress. When he is unable to repay it, Shylock takes him to a court of law. The battle between Shylock and the lawyer Balthasar (Portia in disguise) is at one level a debate between those who stand by 'the letter of the law' and those prepared to show mercy. It is too simple to say that this is a battle between Jewish and Christian ideas. Shakespeare shows how both sides lock themselves into a merciless struggle for revenge.

In a sense this is an extension of the debate about trade. The 16th century saw a significant shift in English law. Medieval law was a system in which compromise was rarely possible and justice went to the one with the best case. Now new practices were developing, more suited to the intricacies of trade. The absolute right to justice could be mitigated – the harsh effects of a law could be reduced through agreement.

Shylock refuses to compromise, but it is clear that he has been driven into this position because he is otherwise without power. The strict letter of justice is all he can rely on. When that is taken away by Balthasar, he is a broken man.

Third, *The Merchant of Venice* looks at what it means to be an outsider. It explores the possibility of toleration. The play appears to be anti-Semitic because so many of its characters hate Jews. We have no grounds for believing that Shakespeare agreed with them. The Christians of Venice bay after Shylock like a pack of wolves. But each time he appears (and he is in only 6 of the 20 scenes in the entire play) we see a complex man, both vulnerable and defiant, witty yet calculating. We see, in other words, a man acting out what his situation demands. When the veil lifts and we glimpse other aspects, we see the cost of being an outsider, for whom turning the other cheek is a luxury he cannot afford if he is to survive:

> 'I am a Jew. If you tickle us do we not laugh? If you poison us do we not die? And if you wrong us shall we not revenge?... The villainy you teach me I will execute, and it shall go hard but I will better the instruction.'

The Merchant of Venice, Act 3 Scene 1, lines 54–67

THE HISTORY PLAYS

The other strand of play-writing which Shakespeare was developing in the later 1590s was the history play. The great tetralogy (a set of four plays) with which he had made his name some years earlier had explored the upheaval of the Wars of the Roses and ended with the victory of Queen Elizabeth I's grandfather, King

Henry VII, over King Richard III. Those plays had begun with the death of King Henry V, and now Shakespeare turned to an exploration of how kings prepare for kingship and exercise it when they have it.

For the Middle Ages, the right to rule involved the power to rule: the king should be the strongest of the nobles – a weak king was likely to be overthrown. But there was also the problem of succession: that kingship should pass from father to son. As Shakespeare had shown in his plays about Henry VI, Edward IV and Richard III, political (and therefore economic and moral) stability depended on closing the gap between might and right, making sure that the rightful ruler had the means of overcoming opposition.

In *King John*, probably written in 1595 or 1596, Shakespeare focuses on this idea of legitimacy by showing the struggle between King John and another claimant to the throne – Philip Falconbridge, the Bastard, an illegitimate son of Richard I. Philip may be the man best fitted to be king but he is barred from the throne by John because his father was not married to his mother. However, John's own weak right to be king unleashes disorder in the land.

King John introduces a second idea that is crucial to the history plays *Richard II*, *Henry IV Parts 1 and 2* and *Henry V*, which intertwine the two crucial concerns for political stability: power and legitimacy. Shakespeare connects the two through a single question: 'Who is my father?' which is not only a political one – 'Who gives me the right to be what I am?' – and a moral one – 'Who do I want to be like?' – but also a practical one – 'How shall I present myself?'

Probably written in 1595, *Richard II* shows a king at war within himself. He has the right to be king but his unlawful actions, in banishing those who oppose him and confiscating their possessions, leads to a rebellion in which he is deposed and eventually murdered by Henry Bolingbroke (now Duke of Lancaster) who has a weaker right to rule, but the might to control the kingdom. Victory in battle, however, makes Bolingbroke 'legitimate':

> **York:** Great Duke of Lancaster, I come to thee
> From plume-plucked Richard, who with willing soul
> Adopts thee heir, and his high sceptre yields
> To the possession of thy royal hand.
> Ascend his throne, decending now from him,
> And long live Henry, of that name the fourth!
>
> *Richard II*, Act 4 Scene I, lines 98–103

Bolingbroke may now be legitimate, but he is a troubled man. His last words in the play are full of guilt for what he has done:

> 'Lords, I protest my soul is full of woe
> That blood should sprinkle me to make me grow...
> I'll make a voyage to the Holy Land
> To wash this blood off from my guilty hand.'
>
> *Richard II*, Act 5 Scene 6, lines 45–50

Richard II takes place entirely in the world of court politics. With the two plays of *Henry IV* Shakespeare takes us on a journey through England, palaces and taverns, country gardens and battlefields. He also introduces one of his most famous characters, the rollickingly overweight and immortally immoral Sir John Falstaff. (Falstaff was to prove so popular that he was reborn in 1597 in the comedy *The Merry Wives of*

100

Windsor, probably written for the celebrations following Lord Chamberlain[†] Hunsdon's installation as a Knight of the Garter[†] at Windsor.) In the earliest performances of *Henry IV*, Falstaff was called Sir John Oldcastle, a historical figure – though not with Falstaff's character. The name was changed under pressure from Oldcastle's descendants, the Cobham family, one of whom was Lord Chamberlain between August 1596 and March 1597 – this probably dates the first performance of *Part 1* to the first half of 1596.

The change from the austerity of *Richard II* to the wide range of the *Henry* plays is not simply to make them more entertaining. Henry IV's son, Prince Hal, who will legitimately be king because his father is, has still to make crucial decisions about what sort of king he will be, which means what sort of man he will be. These choices are dramatized in the triangular relationship between Henry, Hal and Falstaff.

Hal moves between the guilt-ridden Henry, weighed down by the affairs of state, from whom he can learn about responsibility and duty, and the alternative court of Falstaff and his disreputable cronies at the Boar's Head Tavern. Falstaff appears at times to be a lovable rogue, and young Prince Hal enjoys his company. But it gradually becomes clear that the older man is a criminal, a man without honour and with no respect for the law or for other people.

As he experiences England in all its variety, so the young prince is brought to the great moment of choice: will he be like Henry or like Falstaff – who will be his true father?

The choice is made more urgent by another rebellion. Powerful families from the North and from Wales want to overthrow Henry. Young Harry Percy, also known as Hotspur, is the most charismatic of the rebels and prompts another triangular relationship. Henry cannot help but see Hotspur as the son he would have preferred, and Hal is all too aware how his father feels. How a child lives up to a parent's expectations is no less a pressing issue in the plays.

All of these matters are focused on one great scene towards the end of *Part 2* when the king, close to death, prepares to pass the crown on to his son. With dramatic effect the physical crown – a visible sign of the anxieties that press upon any king – passes between king and prince. First Hal removes it without permission from the sleeping king. When Henry wakes he is furious that the crown has been taken, believing that Hal's links with Falstaff will prevent him from ruling wisely:

'...the fifth Harry from curbed licence plucks
The muzzle of restraint, and the wild dog
Shall flesh his tooth on every innocent.'

Henry IV Part 2, Act 4 Scene 3, lines 259–261

But Hal has already recognized which way he must turn. He will change and be Henry's son – picking up the responsibilities of the kingdom. Shakespeare shows that choice in its starkest terms in the final scene. Hal has been crowned Henry V. Falstaff comes, begging favours for himself and his friends, but the new king crushes him:

102

'I know thee not, old man. Fall to thy prayers...
Presume not that I am the thing I was,
For God doth know, so shall the world perceive,
That I have turned away my former self.'

Henry IV Part 2, Act 5 Scene 5, lines 47, 56–58

Kings are known by how they show themselves to the world. Kings and queens are actors, always in role, always presenting themselves as in a play. In the history plays Shakespeare reveals a deep understanding of the essence of politics as keeping power by showing power. He shows, too, the inner costs of power and kingship: rulers may be racked by guilt or uncertainty but failing to display their right to rule opens up power vacuums that others will rush in to fill.

Henry V was written in 1599 and is probably the last play Shakespeare wrote for the Lord Chamberlain's Men before they left The Theatre for their new home across the river at The Globe. It is often seen as a triumphant celebration of English greatness, a propaganda piece, but we should know Shakespeare better by now. It shows rebellion, uncertainty, error, arrogance and the horrors of war. Henry V is the man who was Prince Hal, aware of his wild youth and aware, too, of his father's pain and guilt.

Henry is good at presenting himself to the public as a king – magnificently able to display his power. But he has a private side too, just like his father. On the night before the battle of Agincourt he disguises himself and goes around the camp listening to his soldiers. They are afraid. Joining a small group he tries to lift them by saying that the coming battle will be for a just cause, so they need not fear death. One of the soldiers,

Michael Williams, answers him:

> 'But if the cause be not good, the King himself hath a
> heavy reckoning to make, when all those legs and arms
> and heads chopped off in a battle shall join together at
> the latter day... I am afeard there are few die well that
> die in battle... Now if these men do not die well, it will be
> a black matter for the King that led them to it...'
>
> *Henry V*, Act 2 Scene 1, lines 133–144

Later, when Henry is alone, he admits to himself what
it really means to be a ruler. In words that recall his
father's agony ('Uneasy lies the head that wears a
crown', *Henry IV Part 2*, Act 3 Scene 1, line 31) he
acknowledges:

> ''Tis not the balm the sceptre and the ball,
> The sword, the mace the crown imperial...
> The throne he sits on, nor the tide of pomp
> That beats upon the high shore of this world –
> No, not all these, laid in bed majestical,
> Can sleep so soundly as the wretched slave...'
>
> *Henry V*, Act 4 Scene 1, lines 257–265

8
THE GLOBE

By the end of 1598 William Shakespeare was a highly successful player and playwright with the Lord Chamberlain's Men, who had themselves become one of the two most important companies in London. Their only serious opposition at this time were the Admiral's Men, still based at Philip Henslowe's playhouse, The Rose, on the south bank of the Thames.

Shakespeare's success was shown in his increasing wealth and status, and almost certainly contributed to an improvement in the Shakespeare family fortunes. In the late 1560s John Shakespeare had applied for a coat-of-arms, a public sign of status. The decline of his business had made him unable to pursue the application, but in October 1596, it was granted. John Shakespeare was described as a man worth some £5000 – a small fortune at a time when a labourer earned about 4 shillings† a week. His application for a coat-of-arms was granted and the motto *Non Sanz Droict* (old French for 'Not Without Right') may have been attached. There is no evidence that the family ever used the motto, although Shakespeare's colleague Ben Jonson in his play *Every Man Out of His Humour* of 1599 (in which Shakespeare very possibly acted) gives a character who has bought his coat-of-arms, with the motto 'Not Without Mustard'. Is this a parody of Shakespeare's?

The granting of a coat-of-arms to the family was presumably assisted by Shakespeare's wealth – not only in supporting his father's financial improvement but also in processing the application. It was small comfort, though, in the context of his loss of his son Hamnet, who died in August 1596.

However, the next year Shakespeare reinforced the family's, and his own, status by buying the second largest house in Stratford: New Place and its garden, at the corner of Chapel Street and Chapel Lane and near the Guild Chapel. It is estimated that he paid one William Underhill about £120 for the property. Five years later he bought a cottage in Chapel Lane and a considerable amount of land just outside the town, as well as making other investments in Stratford during the following years. These various deals would have made him a very substantial figure in Stratford affairs.

There is one small but satisfying coincidence hidden in these deals. Before the bailiff† and aldermen† of Stratford had been given responsibility for the repair of the bridge over the river in the 1550s, the costs of its upkeep had been provided by the proceeds from the performance of an annual play of St George and the Dragon. In 1598 Shakespeare provided stone from New Place, unwanted during rebuilding work, for the repair of the bridge. Once more work on Stratford's bridge was funded by plays.

In London, in the meantime, the Lord Chamberlain's Men were undergoing a time of change. The lease on The Theatre was due to run out and the company was in dispute with the owner of the land, Giles Allen. Their situation was not helped when playing companies suddenly ran out of favour with the authorities after a play called *The Isle of Dogs* appeared to be making fun of the royal court. The actors responsible were a new group called Pembroke's Men performing at The Swan, which was in the Liberty† of the Manor of Paris Gardens, on the south bank of the river. The Swan had been built in 1595 by Francis Langley, a sharp city financier. It was sited very near The Rose, in a clear attempt to steal its audience. Pembroke's Men had probably been established to be its resident company.

The offence caused by *The Isle of Dogs* had an immediate but only short-term effect on the other companies, and they were soon back in action. However, the dispute with Giles Allen was rumbling on and the Lord Chamberlain's Men moved out of The Theatre and played for a short time at The Curtain nearby. By the end of 1598 it was clear that no agreement with Allen was going to be found. The landlord having threatened to demolish the playhouse, desperate measures were needed. It appears that the Lord Chamberlain's Men found a legal loophole which would allow them to remove the building from the site. And so on 28 December 1598, Richard Burbage and his brother Cuthbert, their mother, a carpenter, a builder and about 12 labourers set to work dismantling The Theatre on its site to the north of the city and took it, piece by piece, through the streets and over the river to a site not far from The Rose and The Swan, where they began to rebuild it. The new playhouse was finished before May 1599 and Henslowe's account books show that it was already a dangerous rival. With the takings at The Rose substantially down, Henslowe and Edward Alleyn themselves decided to move – back north of the river. Their new theatre, called The Fortune, was in the Liberty of Finsbury between the present Whitecross Street and Golden

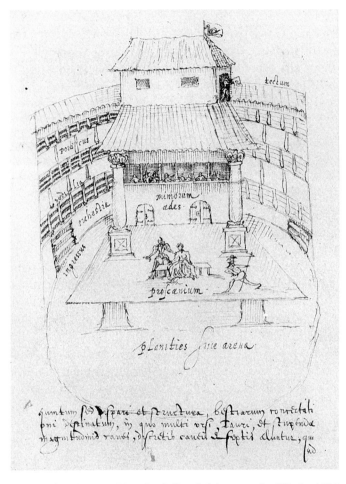

A copy by Arnout Van Buchell of Johannes de Witt's 1596
drawing of The Swan theatre.

Lane (where there is still a Fortune Street). The Fortune was constructed in 1600 and was built by Peter Streete, who had helped the Burbages dismantle The Theatre and build their new playhouse. Possibly in an attempt to revive the Admiral's Men in their new playhouse, Edward Alleyn made a brief return to the stage.

The new playhouse of the Lord Chamberlain's Men was called The Globe, and with that name a further Shakespearean motif comes into focus. The flag which flew above the stage bore the Latin motto, *Totus Mundus Agit Histrionem*, which you could translate as 'All the world's a stage'. We are once more back in the world of resemblances. The play of *Henry V* had incorporated a character known as Chorus[†], who sets the scene for the action and comments on it. Part of his function is to point up the resemblance and the difference between the action of history and the action of the play:

> '...pardon, gentles all,
> The flat unraisèd spirits that hath dared
> On this unworthy scaffold to bring forth
> So great an object. Can this cock-pit hold
> The vasty fields of France? Or may we cram
> Within this wooden O the very casques
> That did affright the air at Agincourt?'
>
> *Henry V*, Act I Scene I, lines 8–14

The questions of Chorus invite the answer 'Yes, we can' so long as one extra ingredient is present:

> 'And let us... on your imaginary forces work...
> Think, when we talk of horses, that you see them...'

Imagination: the creator of resemblances, and with that, the bringer about of transformation. As Duke Theseus said of the players towards the end of *A Midsummer Night's Dream*:

> 'The best in this kind are but shadows, and the worst are no worse if imagination amend them.'

And Hippolyta ironically responds:

> 'It must be your imagination, then, and not theirs.'
>
> *A Midsummer Night's Dream*, Act 5 Scene 1, lines 210-212

Players and playgoers shared in making a playhouse a place of the imagination.

GOING TO THE GLOBE

> 'After dinner on the 21st September, at about two o'clock, I went with my companions over the water, and in the strewn roof-house saw the tragedy[i] of the first Emperor Julius with at least fifteen characters very well acted. At the end of the comedy they danced according to their custom, with extreme elegance. Two in men's clothes and two in women's gave this performance, in wonderful combination with each other.'

This account by Thomas Platter, a Swiss visitor to London, is of an early performance of *Julius Caesar* at The Globe. Some scholars think this was the play with which the Lord Chamberlain's Men opened the new playhouse, but since we know The Globe was completed (or very nearly) by May 1599, this seems unlikely. Others suggest that *Henry V*, a suitably spectacular play, or *As You Like It*, with its famous speech beginning 'All the world's a stage', are possible candidates. We don't really know how the Lord Chamberlain's Men chose to open their new playhouse, but a combination of Platter's account and other evidence, including those of the plays themselves, gives us a good deal of valuable information about how The Globe was built, financed and used.

The Globe used the timbers of The Theatre and so probably shared much of the older theatre's basic construction. It was probably a 20-sided polygon, which would make it look almost circular, and was somewhere between 27 and 30 metres in diameter. It had a thatched roof (Platter's 'strewn roof-house'). We do not know what The Globe looked like inside. It would have had a raised stage – we don't really know the size but if other playhouses of the time are anything to go by it was about 13.5 metres wide by 7.5 metres deep, into the audience. The area in front of the stage would be for standing customers, while two galleries on three sides contained benches or seats for wealthier playgoers. Behind the stage was the tiring house† – for costume changes, props, scenery and as a general gathering place for the company.

The Globe, like the other playhouses, was a very flexible playing place. The tiring house contained machinery enabling special effects or even actors to be 'flown' in (suspended on ropes and lowered to the stage or allowed to hang in the air), the stage had trap-doors for quick exits and entrances, there were balconies for lovers, battlements for soldiers, and alcoves across which curtains could be drawn. Its open stage could be a room or the sea, a wood or a city street. Above all, it was an intimate enclosed space which focused attention on the stage and allowed the imagination to take flight.

A self-portrait by Richard Burbage (1567–1619), the King's Men's chief actor and the first performer of such roles as Hamlet and King Lear.

Old James Burbage had died in 1597 and the dealings with Giles Allen about the lease on The Theatre had been carried out by his sons Cuthbert and Richard. They probably negotiated the agreement to lease the land on the Bankside for the new playhouse, but when it was signed seven men were named as sharers† in The Globe, which presumably was extended into the arrangements about profit-sharing. One half-share went to Cuthbert and Richard Burbage between them, while the other half was divided between five of the Lord Chamberlain's Men: Thomas Pope, Augustine Phillips, John Heminges, the clown Will Kemp and William Shakespeare. To be a sharer in the takings from a playhouse was another step towards considerable wealth. The group changed over the years, of course, and the shares changed hands. For instance, Thomas Pope died in 1604 and Will Kemp left the company before the end of 1599 and went freelance. There is evidence to suggest he was never happy in a company and preferred to strike out on his own.

Kemp was a clown famous for his jigs†. He had probably created the roles of Bottom in *A Midsummer Night's Dream* and Costard in *Love's Labour's Lost*, for instance. It is likely he made his name as a court jester for the Earl of Leicester – and was more like a stand-up comic than a company man. After leaving the Lord Chamberlain's Men, he undertook a marathon solo 'dance' from London to Norwich and wrote a book about it, but died, in poverty and probably from the plague†, in 1603.

There is no obvious clown's role for Kemp in *Julius Caesar* and so it is possible he had already stopped working at The Globe by September 1599. Platter remarks that the jig was performed by 'two men and two women' (presumably men dressed as women), which might suggest that Kemp was not one of them, but the fact that there was a jig at all might argue for his presence.

The jig which traditionally ended the plays – like a bawdy version of the choreographed curtain-calls which often end musicals today – was a popular part of the event for Elizabethan playgoers. Kemp was a favourite in such performances. But it appears that, as tastes changed, the jigs, while continuing at the more down-market theatres such as The Curtain or, often, The Fortune, ceased to be a part of the offerings of the more serious playhouses.

And certainly The Globe seems to have set out to establish itself as a playhouse suited to the morality and taste of what might be called a more discerning audience. From 1599 Shakespeare's plays begin to adopt a different tone, which may in part represent an attempt to develop a different playgoing market.

The world/stage resemblance undoubtedly contributes to this new tone. If 'all the world's a stage', then there may be some comfort to see on stage a world that is ordered, in which, no matter what confusions reign, everything turns out well in the end. Unfortunately for that line of argument – one that wants to make Shakespeare as comfortable a playwright as he was perhaps becoming economically – while many of his plays can be read in that way, in performance they become decidedly ambiguous: by the end no one is wholly good (or unequivocally bad), no one completely happy, nothing absolutely certain. This, too, is a product of resemblance: when something is only like something else (for example when the pairing off of the lovers at the end of *Twelfth Night* only appears to be a happy ending), there is always room for doubt.

JULIUS CAESAR

The opening of *Julius Caesar* is a tremendous shock. A crowd comes tumbling onto the stage in carnival mood. They are sent packing, but all through the play the energy of the crowd and danger of the mob are never far away. In the late 1590s economic unrest and rebellion were in the air, and by 1599 the government and the city of London authorities were deeply suspicious of large gatherings. This is undoubtedly one of the reasons for attempts to ban players' performances, and Shakespeare does not hesitate to show wealthy citizens what they were most afraid of. After Caesar has been killed the same carnival crowd turns into a lynch-mob and tears Cinna the poet to pieces.

Shakespeare's use of the crowd in *Julius Caesar* is complex. The play is set in Ancient Rome at a time when its citizens were trying to find ways of controlling powerful individuals and families. A republic had been established to share power between different sections of the community, but there were those who feared that Julius Caesar's victorious return from war might give him an excuse to be proclaimed emperor, returning Rome to the bad old days of tyranny and cruelty. Will Caesar's ambition mean the end of the Roman republic? Two Romans, Cassius and Brutus, are afraid that it will, and arrange a secret meeting with others of the same view. Together they decide that Caesar must die, if the republic is to survive.

Here, then, is another crowd – a mob, even – in the middle of Rome. The conspirators may be noblemen and senators, but how different are they from the rabble who will kill Cinna? As the conspirators debate between themselves we are back in the middle of the Shakespearean motif of language and silence. Language persuades and may drive us into action but after the words there is only the silence of the dead Caesar and the dead Cinna.

There are differences between Cassius and Brutus which highlight this motif. Brutus is an idealist – he is committed to the Roman ideal of republicanism and opposed to Caesar because he threatens that ideal. As they debate, it becomes clear that Cassius's persuasive tongue hides less pure motives: there is some of Caesar's pride and ambition in him too.

After the conspirators have killed Caesar they realize they need to persuade the people – the crowd – that they have acted in the crowd's best interests. Brutus addresses them and appears to win them over:

> 'Romans, countrymen, and lovers, hear me for my
> cause, and be silent that you may hear...
> Who is here so rude that would not be a Roman?...
> Who is here so vile that will not love his country?'
>
> *Julius Caesar*, Act 3 Scene 1, lines 13, 30, 32

Brutus's speech is a model of persuasive political oratory[†]. Shakespeare writes it in prose as though to reinforce his directness and idealism. After he has finished, Caesar's close friend Mark Antony approaches the conspirators and asks to address the crowd, promising to reinforce Brutus's arguments. Cassius is reluctant, but Brutus agrees. Mark Antony's famous speech, in verse, with many rhetorical[†] flourishes, plays on ideas of ambition and honour, appears to applaud the conspirators but ends with a frank appeal to the greed of the mob and turns them into a pack howling for the blood of Brutus and Cassius. Under the cover of reasonable argument he whips up emotion, moving from

> '[Brutus] Hath told you Caesar was ambitious
> ...And Brutus is an honourable man'

through

> 'I fear I wrong the honourable men
> Whose daggers have stabbed Caesar...'

to, with heavy irony,

> 'I am no orator as Brutus is,
>   But were I Brutus,
> And Brutus Antony, there were an Antony
> Would ruffle up your spirits, and put a tongue
> In every wound of Caesar that should move
> The stones of Rome to rise and mutiny.'
>
> *Julius Caesar*, Act 3 Scene 2, lines 78–79, 88, 152–153, 212, 221–225

Antony's speech is a superb example of rhetoric: highly patterned, complex language, appearing to say one thing while all the time implying something else, appealing to the emotions rather than reason and, in its typically Shakespearean master-stroke, relying on silence to make its most telling point when he uncovers the bloody body of Caesar. The boy from Stratford grammar school[†] had learned his lessons about the arts of persuasion well.

Within the rhetoric of drama, Antony's speech is a highly dramatic act: it addresses the crowds and changes their allegiance and at the very same time addresses the playgoer, drawing us into the crowd in Ancient Rome. The stage of The Globe was suited to such a double action. The actor playing Antony could come close to the playgoers standing in front of the stage – standing like a crowd, not seated like an audience – and address them directly. It was such power as this that made the city authorities fear the playhouses. And at the end, while staying true to the story, Shakespeare leaves his audience (the wealthier ones sitting safely in the galleries) no comfort. The careful idealist Brutus dies, the rabble-rousing Antony takes power.

In *Julius Caesar* the crowd, which so easily becomes a mob, is a dangerous frame surrounding the political debates at the play's heart. They are a stark reminder that politics is the art of manipulating unreason more than that of marshalling good arguments.

AS YOU LIKE IT

Another candidate for the first play that may have been performed at The Globe returns us to a mysterious wood. This wood is both in the Ardennes in France and the very English Forest of Arden (the name for the area to the north and west of Stratford). It is a wintry landscape peopled not with fairies and amateur actors but with outlaws. *As You Like It* is one of those plays that have suffered particularly from the tendency to make Shakespeare's work romantic and pretty – in fact it is a tough exploration of love which makes much of the contrast between town and country, power misused and resisted.

The world portrayed in *As You Like It* is close to

economic, social and moral collapse. There is poverty and famine, while brothers are stealing the inheritance of brothers. Recent scholarship has shown that it mirrors a time in the late 1590s when a series of disastrous harvests raised social tension. We know that the Forest of Arden was a violent place in the 1590s, full of poverty, feuding, outlaws and assaults as the impact of economic change bit deep into the countryside. *As You Like It* is full of the conventions of plays and poems about shepherds and shepherdesses dancing under blue skies, but the reality is quite different and summed up in the song of Amiens, a lord who has become an outlaw:

'Blow, blow thou winter wind,
Thou art not so unkind
  As man's ingratitude.
Thy tooth is not so keen,
Because thou art not seen,
  Although thy breath be rude.
Hey-ho, sing hey-ho, unto the green holly.
Most friendship is feigning, most loving, mere folly.
  Then hey-ho, the holly;
  This life is most jolly.'

As You Like It, Act 2 Scene 7, lines 175–184

This, then, is the frame within which Shakespeare paints a picture of different sorts of love and friendship. At the beginning of the play we see two destructive relationships between brothers: Duke Frederick has usurped the land of his brother, Duke Senior, and banished him into the forest; Orlando, the youngest son of Duke Frederick's old enemy Sir Rowland de Bois, is in turn being ill-treated by his older brother, Oliver, and he too escapes into the forest. Contrasted

119

with this are faithful friendships: between Orlando and his old servant Adam; and between Rosalind, Duke Senior's daughter, and Celia, the daughter of Duke Frederick.

Rosalind and Orlando fall in love but Rosalind, disguised as a boy (for safety in the dangerous forest), puts him through what is best seen as an education in the practicalities of love, friendship and marriage, before they are united. Other pairs of lovers meet in the forest – there is the romantic affair of Silvius and Phoebe, and the uncomplicated relationship between Touchstone, another urban character out of place in the forest, and the countrygirl Audrey – before everything is resolved, Duke Senior and Orlando are returned to their rightful places in society, and the lovers prepare for marriage under the watchful eye of Hymen, god of marriage. The play does not quite end there, however. One of the men banished to the forest with Duke Senior is Jaques, whose serious temperament regularly reminds the others that the world is full of pain, and that joys are short-lived. It is he who speaks of the world being a stage:

> 'And all the men and women merely players.
> They have their exits and their entrances...'
>
> *As You Like It*, Act 2 Scene 7, lines 140–141

After Hymen has blessed the marriages, Jaques offers a more sober assessment of what awaits the pairs of lovers – then goes to live as a hermit in the forest:

> 'So, to your pleasures;
> I am for other than for dancing measures.'
>
> *As You Like It*, Act 5 Scene 4, lines 190–191

THE MASTER OF THE REVELS

The Lord Chamberlain's Men had a particularly close relationship with those officials whose job was not only to provide entertainments for the queen and her court but also to censor every play before it could be performed: making sure it contained nothing likely to offend the queen or her friends and allies.

The Lord Chamberlain[†] was the chief officer of the court responsible for everyone who might come into contact with the queen in her palaces. This included those who served at table and assisted in her private quarters, who looked after her clothes and jewels, the upkeep of the palaces, her collections of weapons, her spiritual well-being (the clergy and choir of the Chapel Royal), as well as musicians, physicians, library staff, gardeners, and masters of the various packs of hunting dogs. The Lord Chamberlain also arranged the royal entertainments and, although a good deal of this work was given to officials known as the Revels Office, he undoubtedly took an active interest, especially if the queen was likely to be present at an event.

During Queen Elizabeth's reign, Shakespeare's company worked for three Lord Chamberlains: Henry Carey, 1st Lord Hunsdon, who held the office between 1585 and 1596, and created the Lord Chamberlain's Men in 1594 after the final demise of the Queen's Men; William Brooke, Lord Cobham, from 1596 to1598; and Henry Carey's son, George, 2nd Lord Hunsdon, who was Chamberlain from 1598 until the queen's death in 1603. It was George Carey's brother, Richard, who rode at speed from London to Edinburgh to be the first to tell James the news that he was now King of England.

The Revels Office consisted of a Master of the Revels[†], one or two clerks and a Yeoman. At first the Yeoman was a tailor, and his job was to maintain the wardrobe of clothes in good order. Later he seems to have played more of a part in getting court performances ready. In 1599 the Yeoman was Edward Kirkham. The Revels Office organized and paid for court performances by playing companies, maintained a collection of costumes, props and scenery, and generally oversaw the London theatre scene. They licensed plays, companies and, eventually, playhouses. In theory, nothing happened on the stage of a London playhouse that had not been agreed with the Master of the Revels.

The first Master with whom Shakespeare would have worked was Sir Edmund Tilney. He had been responsible for gathering together the Queen's Men in 1583 and remained in office until 1607 when he was succeeded by his nephew Sir George Buc. Licensing involved a fee which, in true Elizabethan and Jacobean[†] fashion, helped increase the wealth of the official issuing the licence. Tilney gradually raised his fees to 7 shillings for a new play (the equivalent of 84 one-penny standing places in a playhouse) and required the companies to pay 5 shillings for every week their playhouse was open. Sir George Buc's fees went up to £1 for issuing a licence which allowed a play to be performed and another £1 for permission to print it. On the other hand, playing companies called to perform before the queen may have earned as much as £10 for a show – probably the equivalent of no more than one full house in an outdoor theatre, but they had the prestige of being at court and the added luxury of being warm and dry.

MASQUES[†]

As well as authorizing companies to perform, the Revels Office also managed the costly productions known as masques, which became increasingly popular during the reign of James I. A masque was a lavish entertainment of music, dance and words. It involved elaborate staging and was very expensive to produce. Ladies and gentlemen of the court often took part – the only theatrical performances where women were accepted on stage – though professional players and musicians are likely to have been involved as well. The architect and designer Inigo Jones was a famous creator of the visual elements of masques, and many were written by Shakespeare's fellow-playwright, Ben Jonson. We have no record of any being written by Shakespeare, though it is quite likely that he was called to participate in them as a member of the Lord Chamberlain's Men and the King's Men. The stagecraft and formal structure of masques (often on themes from Ancient Greek and Roman mythology suitably doctored to heap praise on King James) did however influence Shakespeare. Many of his plays after about 1605 include scenes of formal dancing or song, sometimes involving mythical characters, who interrupt, but also add a deeper layer, to the action.

CENSORSHIP

As well as organizing events at court and earning money by issuing licences, the Revels Office had an important censorship function. The opportunity for players to give offence or make libellous, blasphemous or treasonable statements on stage was always an anxiety for Tudor governments, and has remained so for governments ever since. Censorship in the British theatre only ended in 1968.

Censorship of plays and players probably began for the 16th-century government as a way of preventing the Corpus Christi[†] plays from becoming a focus for Catholic[†] sympathizers. It developed in two ways. First, to ensure that only appropriate plays would be presented at court (Sir Edmund Tilney's original function seems to have been to ensure that the queen got acceptable entertainment as cheaply as possible). And second, to reinforce state control over information in order to minimize the risk of dissent and rebellion. Nevertheless by the 1590s there was a clear structure. Playing companies were required to submit new work to the Master of the Revels, who would (for a fee) read it, make notes on it and send it back to them with his instructions to make necessary changes, without which no licence to perform would be issued.

Sometime in the early 1590s a group of playwrights collaborated on a play about Sir Thomas More, Lord Chancellor in the government of Henry VIII. More opposed the king's divorce from Catherine of Aragon and was eventually executed. The play was submitted to Tilney who clearly thought that it was politically unacceptable, and he asked for a considerable number of changes to be made. It is unclear what happened next, but it seems most likely that the play was put away for a few years and only brought out again after the queen died in 1603. Tilney's notes are a fascinating insight into the boundaries players might not cross:

'Leave out the insurrection wholy & the Cause ther off & begin with Sr Tho: Moore at the mayors sessions with a reportt afterwardes off his

good service don being Shrive [Sheriff] of London uppon a mutiny
Agaynst the Lumbardes only by A shortt reporte & nott otherwise at
your own perilles.'

E. Tilney

In other words, the players had to cut out the scenes
that showed riots against foreigners (there were similar riots in London in the 1590s – the scenes might
have inflamed an already dangerous situation). Later
in the play they were told to cut out the scene where
More refuses to obey the king. But Tilney did not try
to ban the play altogether, although it showed a
Catholic martyr – he offered suggestions for changing
it to make it acceptable. Plays could take risks but only
up to a point. The play of *Sir Thomas More* includes
two scenes which may have been written by
Shakespeare. It still exists in manuscript form and it is
possible that one section is in his own handwriting.
The scene is precisely that showing the riots against
foreigners but, if it is by Shakespeare, we don't know
whether he wrote it before submission to Tilney (and
so incurred his displeasure), or for the revisions after
the death of Queen Elizabeth (and so ignored Tilney's
demands).

By the time *Julius Caesar* and *As You Like It* were
being performed at The Globe, Shakespeare was nearly 36 years old, an experienced actor and playwright
and a successful and increasingly wealthy businessman. Having learned their trade in a number of playing companies from the 1580s onwards, he and his
fellow players in the Lord Chamberlain's Men had
progressed to being one of the two most successful
companies in London, with regular performances at
the royal court and a certain amount of touring

125

around the country. With success was going not only wealth but also the opportunity for increased professionalism. The players were highly skilled – the system of apprenticeships[†] ensured that young actors were well trained – and staging techniques were becoming increasingly subtle. Writers were responding to these new possibilities by creating increasingly complex situations, and new styles of play were in turn demanding new responses from actors. They were learning to walk with greater assurance the narrow path between royal favour and censorship, between popularity with a wide audience and the refined atmosphere of the court.

9
THE KING'S MEN

We have already seen in Chapter 1 how, in May 1603, the Lord Chamberlain's Men received a royal warrant and became the King's Men. Queen Elizabeth's Lord Chamberlain†, George Carey, had ceremonially broken his white stick of office on her death, and whatever his hopes for re-appointment, he was replaced by Thomas Howard, shortly to be made Earl of Suffolk. Under Howard, and Sir George Buc, Master of the Revels†, the new company's relationship with the court developed. King James was a great believer in displaying the magnificence of his court, and he expected the plays chosen for his entertainment to be spectacular. But he also loved intellectual arguments, and wanted his plays to be interesting explorations of ideas. We also saw in Chapter 1 how the King's Men responded to this new atmosphere, and how it was coloured, for Shakespeare, by a deeper cynicism. Already in what were to prove the last years of Queen Elizabeth, a sense of decay had begun to creep into his work. The framework of death and disorder within which he had set many of his comedies and love stories increasingly coloured the plots of love and friendship; the political awareness, already so acute in the history plays, became even more intricate examinations of the gap between words and actions, between public statements and private intentions.

We have some information about Shakespeare's own business affairs during these years. As a sharer† in the Chamberlain's Men and King's Men he had his cut of the profits not only from the plays but also from the takings at The Globe. In addition he was keeping links with Stratford, and we know of a number of business deals in which he was involved at this time.

The attack on Shakespeare in *Greene's Groatsworth of Wit* in 1592 had accused him, amongst other things, of being a money-lender and a hoarder (see page 36 & 58). Later events may show that attack to have some substance.

During 1598 two fellow citizens of Stratford, Abraham Sturley and Richard Quiney, were in London on Stratford business, and they were in debt. Richard, in London, received advice from his father, Adrian Quiney, back in Stratford. The old man suggested that his son should 'bargain with Mr Sha.' (i.e. with William Shakespeare) for a loan and, if successful, he should use anything left over after paying off the debt to buy stockings at Evesham market for their shop. Quiney, staying at the Bell Inn in Carter Lane near St Paul's Cathedral, wrote to Shakespeare on 25 October begging his help:

> 'Loving Countryman, I am bold of you as a Friend, craving your help with xxxli [i.e. £30]...You shall Friend me much in helping me out of all the debts I owe in London... You shall neither lose credit nor money by me... and if we bargain further you shall be paymaster yourself... My time bids me hasten to an end... I fear I shall not be back this night from the court. Haste...'

The letter was possibly not sent and disappeared into Quiney's papers, where it was preserved. Did Quiney bump into Shakespeare before he could do so? Or did Shakespeare return it with his reply? Whatever happened to the letter, it appears that Shakespeare promised to help them obtain the money they needed. Sturley wrote to Quiney on 4 November alluding to a promise but looking for sight of the hard cash:

'...our countryman Mr Wm Shak, would procure us money, which I will
like of as I shall hear when, and where... and how...'

Quiney and Sturley appear to have approached
Shakespeare because they thought he would have £30
ready money available, or knew where he could lay his
hands on it. Shakespeare may well have taken the
same line that he appears to have taken with Greene
and not used his own money for the loan – perhaps he
distrusted their ability to repay. But he did on this
occasion use contacts to see that his fellow townsmen
would get their money. In the end, though, Quiney's
business at court was successful and his expenses were
paid, but the correspondence opens up a window on
Shakespeare's business dealings and the strength of his
links with Stratford, where he was now a substantial
property owner and investor.

Shakespeare bought New Place in Stratford in May
1597 during a run of bad harvests which were pushing
up grain prices. As always during such times of shortage, those who can afford to do so have a tendency to
hoard what is in short supply – not only to keep themselves stocked up, but also to wait until the shortage
has pushed up prices so that they can sell on some of
their hoard at a profit. In February 1598 a Stratford
survey showed that William Shakespeare was hoard-
ing 10 quarters of malt (used for the brewing of beer)
which was worth about £25 – a labourer at this time
could earn about 4 shillings[†] a week. It was one of the
larger stockpiles in the town. We don't know whether
he was holding the malt for his own home brewing or
in order to sell it at a profit, but it is significant that he
had the spare cash to buy such an amount at all.

Around the time The Globe began to open its doors to the paying public, Shakespeare moved from the London house he owned in St Helen's parish, which was close to The Theatre and The Curtain but not so handy for the playhouses on the south bank of the river, and went to live in the Liberty[†] of the Clink, near The Globe. A number of the Lord Chamberlain's Men seem to have done the same, but, it appears, not Richard Burbage who, at his death in 1619, was still living in Holywell Street, close to the site of the original Theatre.

TWELFTH NIGHT

In early February 1602 a law student at the Middle Temple in London noted in his diary that at their feast on Candlemas (2nd February):

> 'we had a play called *Twelfth Night, or What You Will* A good practice to make the steward believe his lady was in love with him.'

The play had probably been written sometime during 1601 and presents a wonderfully upside-down world where fools are wise and wise men fools, girls are boys and nothing is quite what it seems. There is a serious frame to the play – the plot is set in motion by a ship-wreck, one of the principal characters is in mourning, and there is a cruel, unjust imprisonment near its end – but it is a much less troubled comedy than *As You Like It.*

Twelfth Night – the last day of Christmas, 6 January – was a day of feasting and fooling often led by a 'Lord of Misrule'[†], a child or servant chosen to create disorder. *Twelfth Night* is a play about confusion and about desire. It explores the gap between what people think they want and what they really want, between what they think they are and what they really are.

A shipwrecked girl (Viola) disguises herself as a boy (Cesario) and joins the court of Count Orsino. He is hopelessly in love with the Countess Olivia (who is in mourning for her own dead brother) and sends Cesario with messages for her. Olivia falls in love with Cesario. Olivia has another suitor – Sir Andrew Aguecheek – who is being egged on by her uncle Sir Toby Belch. The steward responsible for running her household is Malvolio, a pompous Puritan[†] who hates fun of every kind. Finally there is Feste, an 'allowed fool' – one with permission to tell the truth, however painful. Belch and his friends trick Malvolio into believing Olivia loves him; he makes a fool of himself and they have him locked up as a madman. Meanwhile Viola's twin brother Sebastian turns up, having escaped drowning. Olivia falls for him, thinking he is Cesario, and they marry. Viola in her turn has fallen in love with Orsino and, in the end, as confusions are unravelled, the two couples marry. The play is full of light hearts and joy but, as so often in Shakespeare's plays, there are uncomfortable undercurrents.

Both Olivia and Viola are mourning for their brothers. Olivia's mourning is so inward-looking that it has lost touch with reality; it takes a good dose of Feste's witty realism to help:

'The more fool, madonna, to mourn for your brother's
soul, being in heaven...

Twelfth Night, Act 1 Scene 5, lines 66–67

Viola is much more realistic, deciding on a plan for her own survival. Her grief is real but she deals with it by beginning to resemble her brother: they were twins and putting on boy's clothes makes her look like him.

This contrast between Olivia's self-love and Viola's love for another runs through the whole play. Olivia is proud and vain; Viola witty, realistic and generous in her attitude to others. Although she is falling in love with Orsino she continues to try to persuade Olivia to marry him. In another key, Malvolio's high opinion of himself constrasts sharply with Antonio (a good friend to Sebastian who turns up alive in Illyria as well to considerable comic confusion). Antonio is a remarkably unselfish friend – he tries to protect Sebastian although it puts him in the greatest personal danger.

As an allowed fool Feste shows far more wisdom and insight than the supposedly wise Malvolio, who is so easily taken in by Toby Belch and his friends.

Finally, the confusions of *Twelfth Night* focus on the uncertainties between boy and girl. Olivia loves Cesario, a boy who is a girl. She meets Sebastian, and she thinks he is Cesario. Viola loves Orsino, but dressed as a boy she cannot declare her love. Although time and patience untangle the knots, we are left with lingering uncertainties: how much did Orsino love the 'boy' Cesario before he knew 'he' was a girl? How much of the girl Viola hiding under the boy Cesario did Olivia fall in love with? How much do the resemblances between boy and girl lead to the truth that we all search for the 'other half' to make us whole – an idea which Shakespeare has already explored in *The Comedy of Errors*. But here he takes the idea further still: how far is each of us both male and female? It is an idea that modern psychology has endorsed but Sebastian says it first:

'You are betrothed both to a maid and man'

Twelfth Night, Act 5 Scene 1, line 261

This ambivalence between man and woman gains even greater force for an audience if we remember that in Shakespeare's time, the players playing the women were themselves boys. From that audience's point of view, they were watching a girl (Viola) played by a boy, pretending to be a boy (Cesario), being loved by Olivia, a woman also played by a boy.

Near the end, Viola and Sebastian find one another at last. And not only are they united, but also Viola and Orsino, Olivia and Sebastian, Sebastian and Antonio, even Sir Toby Belch and the servant Maria. Here are so many different ways in which two separate beings can come together as a single loving whole. The confusions of *Twelfth Night* are over.

But the last word is with Feste, the fool who is so wise. Feste remains alone at the end of the play, singing a sad song. Indeed his presence throughout adds the tones of autumn's dying leaves to the whole play. He has kept his wits while all those around him are losing theirs. He understands, as he sings, that

'Present mirth hath present laughter.
What's to come is still unsure...
Youth's a stuff will not endure.'

Twelfth Night, Act 2 Scene 3, lines 47–8, 51

HAMLET

Somewhere between 1600 and 1602 Shakespeare wrote what has become one of his most famous plays. When it was registered for printing (or at least to prevent anyone else from printing it), on 26 July 1602, it was called *The Revenge of Hamlet Prince of Denmark*. It first appeared in print a year later in a version that was probably based on the imperfect memory of an actor who had played a minor role in the play. In 1604 a further edition claimed to present the play 'according to the true and perfect copy'. This was nearly twice as long as the first edition. It is likely that Shakespeare's own original text (or something like it) was used for the 1604 edition but that the play was further revised as the experience of performing it grew. These later revisions then form the basis of the text in the First Folio[†] edition of 1623, put together by his fellow actors several years after Shakespeare's death.

The play was first advertised as *The Revenge of Hamlet...*, and this gives us an important clue as to its style and meaning. Revenge as a subject is as old as drama itself and as modern as films like *Die Hard*. Ancient Greek and Roman plays frequently use the drive to avenge the death of a parent or a child, or sexual infidelity, as the motive for action and the field of conflict. One of the more immediate models for English tragedy[†] were the plays of Seneca, written in Rome in the 1st century CE, in which complex, highly theatrical and extremely bloody deaths are devised as a punishment for killing. Vendettas pass down from one generation to another and are only resolved by general blood-letting to cleanse families or society of their guilt and bring order out of chaos.

There was a particular vogue for such plays in the 1580s and 1590s. A version of *Hamlet*, probably not by Shakespeare, was performed from at least 1589 onwards, and Christopher Marlowe makes use of the revenge tradition in his play *The Jew of Malta*. Thomas Kyd's *The Spanish Tragedy*, however, was one of the most popular revenge plays. It included a ghost demanding vengeance as well as a 'pretend' play enacted by some of the characters within the main play, while at the end the stage is littered with dead bodies – all recognizable features of *Hamlet*. But Kyd's characters are actors in both senses of the word. They devise the most theatrical means of death possible for their enemies and they grasp the demand to kill with tremendous urgency.

Hamlet is set in the Danish castle of Elsinore. Hamlet's father, the king, has died and his widow, Gertrude, has married the old king's brother, Claudius. Hamlet is unhappy about the speed of his mother's remarriage within two months of his father's death. The ghost of the dead king appears to his son to tell him that he was killed by Claudius, and demands that Hamlet should revenge him. Also at Elsinore is a courtier called Polonius who has a son, Laertes, who leaves for France, and a daughter, Ophelia. Ophelia is in love with Hamlet but he, pretending to be mad as part of his plan to revenge his father, rejects her. Polonius tries to find out what is affecting Hamlet. At the same time Claudius and Gertrude have encouraged Hamlet's old friends, Rosencrantz and Guildenstern, to do the same. But Hamlet will confide in no one. When a band of travelling players arrive at the castle he devises a plot to make Claudius tell the truth.

Hamlet adds some new scenes to a play which the company is to perform before the king. The scenes act out the killing of Hamlet's own father and, when he sees them, Claudius panics. He arranges for Rosencrantz and Guildenstern to take Hamlet away with them to England and have him murdered there.

In the meantime, Hamlet has gone to see his mother, Gertrude, in her bedchamber. Polonius has been speaking with her before Hamlet arrives and he hides behind a large hanging tapestry. Hamlet tries to persuade his mother to give up Claudius. The ghost appears again and Hamlet becomes more and more frenzied, until, hearing a noise behind the tapestry, he lunges with his sword and kills Polonius.

Claudius is trapped between the demands of governing Denmark, caught up in a war, Hamlet's behaviour, and his own increasing guilt. Laertes returns when he hears of his father's death and swears revenge. Ophelia's grief makes her go mad and she drowns herself.

Hamlet escapes on the journey to England, and returns to Denmark, aware now of Claudius's intention to murder him. Claudius tries to bring matters to a head, and a duel is arranged between Hamlet and Laertes. Laertes' sword is to be tipped with poison. In addition, Claudius prepares a poisoned cup of wine for Hamlet. They fight, but things go wrong. Gertrude drinks the poisoned wine, in the confusion of the fight both Laertes and Hamlet are wounded with the poisoned sword and, just before he dies, Hamlet kills Claudius.

Shakespeare's *Hamlet* is a full-blooded revenge play with ghosts, plays-within-plays, the glint of flashing swords and a good deal of blood. But this Hamlet is no actor rushing into vengeance; rather, a man plagued with doubt and indecision. The characters of Kyd's play were often simply sketched in; Shakespeare draws his much more fully. We see their complex motivation; we are shown their own sense of guilt and anxiety; and we see the desire for revenge in the context of a tricky political situation. By a bitter irony, Hamlet bungles just about every killing he tries. Hearing a sound behind a curtain he stabs not his uncle but the old political adviser, Polonius, so setting in train another revenge plot by Laertes, as well as Ophelia's madness. Even the deaths at the end of the play are a mess.

The plot is a chapter of accidents and full of delays and mistakes – just like life. Full of words – the full text of the 1604 edition is 3300 lines long and lasts nearly four hours – these words are a breeding ground for doubt. Words offer opportunities for action, and, at the same time, reasons for not acting:

'To be, or not to be; that is the question;
Whether 'tis nobler in the mind to suffer
The slings and arrows of outrageous fortune,
Or to take arms against a sea of troubles,
And, by opposing, end them...
Thus conscience doth make cowards of us all,
And thus the native hue of resolution
Is sicklied o'er with the pale cast of thought
And enterprises of great pith and moment
With this regard their currents turn awry,
And lose the name of action.'

Hamlet, Act 3 Scene 1, lines 58–62, 85–90

King Claudius comes to be conscience-stricken by his killing of Hamlet's father. Hamlet worries about his conscience before he does anything at all. Words, their meaning, and the way they are the springs of action continue to fascinate Hamlet. When the group of travelling players arrive at Elsinore, Hamlet marvels when one of them declaims a speech about the Ancient Trojan war, full of intense emotion. But Hamlet's feelings cannot push him towards revenge:

'What would he do
Had he the motive and the cue for passion
That I have?... I...
...can say nothing – no, not for a king
Upon whose property and most dear life
A damned defeat was made...
O vengeance!-
Why, what an ass am I? Ay, sure, this is most brave,
That I, the son of the dear murderèd,
Must, like a whore, unpack my heart with words
And fall a-cursing like a very drab*...

Hamlet, Act 2 Scene 2, lines 561–563, 566, 570–572, 583–588

Hamlet arranges for the players to act out a scene which will 'catch the conscience of the king'. He succeeds, up to a point, but the final acts of revenge come about through a different quarrel altogether. None of Hamlet's words have led to actions that will properly avenge the killing of the old king. In the end nothing has worked, and Hamlet, that man most able to express his feelings but able to do precious little with them, dies inarticulately:

---

* drab = a prostitute

'The rest is silence
O, O, O, O.'

Hamlet, Act 5 Scene 2, lines 310–311

If Shakespeare was writing, or revising, *Hamlet* in about 1601, then there is particular poignancy about Hamlet's grief for his father's death: 1601 was the year that John Shakespeare died in Stratford. Whatever his feelings for his father, his death made William considerably richer. We do not know the terms of John Shakespeare's will but as eldest son he would have stood to receive a substantial inheritance of land and property. And is it entirely coincidental that the Prince of Denmark's name recalls Shakespeare's own son, Hamnet, who had died four years earlier? The Prince's name goes back into legend, but the similarity with his dead son's name may have attracted Shakespeare to the subject.

THE DEVELOPMENT OF INDOOR THEATRES

If the tradition of outdoor theatres had grown out of the open-air performances of the Corpus Christi† plays, there was another, no less important, tradition of indoor performances. Playing companies had regularly performed in the halls of great houses as well as the market or guild halls of the towns – as at Stratford. There was also a long tradition of performing in the halls of schools and universities as well as in royal palaces. It should come as no surprise, then, that 1576, which saw the building of the first purpose-built outdoor London playhouse (The Theatre) should also have been the year of the first permanent indoor playhouse in converted monastic buildings at the Blackfriars, on the north bank of the Thames not far from St Paul's Cathedral.

139

This playhouse was set up for a company of boy players[†] under the direction of Richard Farrant, at that time Master of the Children of the Chapel Royal, who provided the choir for the queen's services in her palaces, as they still do today. Farrant established his theatre under false pretences. He had obtained the rooms in the Blackfriars by saying that they were to be used as a school, but in fact converted it into a play-house. Aware of the money to be made from theatrical performances, he made use of the fact that acting was an important part of Elizabethan education, to turn his boys into what was effectively a professional com-pany. Farrant was thrown out of the Blackfriars in 1584 when his landlord, William More, realized what was going on.

Boy players continued to be a significant part of the London playgoing scene. It seems unlikely that Shakespeare himself ever wrote for them – and if some of his comments in *Hamlet* are anything to go by, he maybe didn't think much of their abilities – but they did attract many other leading playwrights. We don't know of many boys who went on to become profes-sional adult actors. Nathan Field, however, who had been with the Children of the Chapel Royal from about 1600, had joined the King's Men by 1616 and rose to be one of its leading players. His father was a Puritan clergyman who preached against plays and players – which must have made their conversations interesting! Field junior was accused of being the father of an illegitimate child in 1619; the mother was Anne, Countess of Argyll.

We know that the Lord Chamberlain's Men were allowed to use the Cross Keys Inn in Gracechurch

Street during the winter of 1598, and probably rooms inside other inns were used from time to time for performances by different companies. Before this, however, in 1596, James Burbage was looking around for an indoor venue. Like Richard Farrant, he settled for the Blackfriars and negotiated with William More for the lease of another part of the old buildings – this time one of the halls. Rather like modern developments in London Docklands or architect-designed accommodation in unused factories, the old Blackfriars monastery had become a fashionable place to live. Perhaps Burbage was trying to attract customers put off by the cold and wet, and by the less fashionable playgoers who turned up at the outdoor playhouses. Whatever his reasons, he reckoned without the Elizabethan version of the present-day 'not in my backyard' syndrome, where people object to developments that might affect their own property or area. Their patron† Henry Carey may have been involved in Burbage's plans – he certainly owned property in the Blackfriars. But after his death, the wealthy families in the Blackfriars (including their late patron†, George Carey, the second Lord Hunsdon) petitioned the government to refuse a licence. Any advantage there might be in bringing a playhouse to the Blackfriars was offset in their view by the fact that it would inevitably bring noisy players and even noisier (and probably plague†-ridden) playgoers too. They were also worried that the playhouse would increase traffic congestion – another objection familiar to us today. Their objections were sustained.

Burbage's plan to attract a different audience had backfired. However, his converted building was used as a playhouse. For the next few years the boy company, the Children of the Chapel Royal (also known as the Children of the Revels), were allowed to return and play there in competition with the boys of St Paul's who had a hall nearer to the Cathedral.

In 1608 the boy players' companies suddenly collapsed in the teeth of Puritan opposition. The Blackfriars became available, and this time the King's Men moved in with (apparently) little opposition. Old father Burbage's wish to see a permanent indoor playhouse had become a reality.

THE BLACKFRIARS THEATRE

There is considerable scholarly argument as to whether moving into an indoor theatre made any appreciable difference to the sort of the plays the King's Men put on, or to the style of their performance. First, players had always worked inside as well as out of doors: on tour and at court, for instance. Second, the companies never got rid of the outdoor venues: they were bigger, and therefore earned them more money; they were a significant part of the style of performing; and they were cheaper to run (the cost of candles for lighting the indoor theatres was very great). Third, the crucial steps in the development of a new type of play – and with it a new, intense, performing style – had already been taken before 1608. However, there can also be no doubt that the intimacy of the indoor playhouses and the opportunity they gave for a different set of special effects (candle-light, the sense of enclosure) widened the range of what was written and how it could be played.

OTHELLO

From about 1602 Shakespeare's plays become increasingly compressed. He no longer spreads the plots across different layers of society but looks more directly at the hidden springs of action in the relationships of a small group of people. There is comedy, but it is often bitter and cynical. The view of the world which the plays present is frequently savage. This trend was to reach a climax with *King Lear*, and we have already seen how it developed from typically Shakespearean themes (love, friendship, separation and loss, betrayal and revenge, the gap between words and actions); in *Othello* we see these themes in their tightest focus.

Othello is the story of a Moor (a north African) who has become a famous soldier leading Venice in its war against the Turks. He is tricked by Iago, his ensign (a junior officer acting as his personal assistant), into falsely believing that his wife, Desdemona, is having an affair with another soldier, Cassio. As Iago works on Othello so he opens a vein of jealousy which the general cannot resist. In the end Othello kills Desdemona. Only then, too late, does he learn the truth, and he kills himself. The strength of the play comes above all from Shakespeare's dissection of the hidden motives and emotions which drive people into action. But he overturns our expectations in a number of ways. First, the general is a Moor – a black man. Just as with Shylock the Jew in *The Merchant of Venice*, Shakespeare takes a figure his audience would regard with suspicion and fear and shows his basic humanity. In the popular imagination blackness was linked with evil – and Shakespeare used this assumption in the character of the wicked Aaron in *Titus Andronicus*. But now he overturns that assumption. Othello is, like King Lear, a man 'more sinned against, than sinning'. Neither his jealous rages nor his bravery are to be attributed to the colour of his skin. Not that Shakespeare ignores the question of prejudice. Desdemona's father, Brabanzio, can have his racism unlocked by Iago:

'Even now, now, very now, an old black ram
Is tupping your white ewe. Arise, arise!
Awake the snorting citizens with the bell,
Or else the devil will make a grandsire of you.'

Othello, Act I Scene I, lines 88–91

And Othello's jealous response is perhaps more easily unlocked because of the Moor's anxiety that he is different; that Desdemona may prefer a white man; that he does not understand her.

Shakespeare overturns our expectations in another way, too. When writing *Othello* he was contributing to a fashion for tragedies[†] which explore the inner motives of men and women, especially their sexual fears and desires. In part these plays develop the revenge tradition – they are generally set in Italy, and involve lurid sexual adventures or threatened loss of innocence. They frequently invoke madness but generally make clear why the characters act as they do. These plays tend, too, to have a wicked manipulator who unleashes the suffering onto innocent victims. But generally there are reasons, however twisted, for what the characters do. In *Othello*, Shakespeare presents us with an essentially motiveless manipulator. Iago offers a whole string of reasons why he is gunning for Othello, but none seems particularly strong. Near the beginning of the play he simply admits, to himself and to us, that he 'hates the Moor' and that is sufficient motivation. At the very end, when reasons for his actions are demanded of him, he responds:

'Demand me nothing. What you know, you know.
From this time forth I never will speak word.'

Othello, Act 5 Scene 2, lines 309–310

At the heart of a play inviting us into the inner lives of its characters, there is a disturbing emptiness. We have seen innocence destroyed, not only Desdemona's but also Othello's, for no other reason than hatred. We see Othello's descent into jealousy and see, too, how these deep and energetic emotions have been unlocked for no reason at all. By stating his intent at the beginning, Iago makes the play one long exercise in dramatic irony†, which reaches its climax in the great scene (Act 3 Scene 3) where he finally traps Othello in his net and turns the general into a raging seeker after blood. We know Iago is tricking Othello, and lying about Desdemona and Cassio, but we can do nothing about it except maybe secretly admire his manipulative skills, pity the deceived Moor and fear for Desdemona. Maybe we fear for ourselves, too. Seeing how the swirling waters of jealousy sweep away Othello, how easily might they overwhelm us?

'Like to the Pontic Sea,
Whose icy current and compulsive course
Ne'er knows retiring ebb, but keeps due on
To the Propontic and the Hellespont,
Even so my bloody thoughts with violent pace
Shall ne'er look back, ne'er ebb to humble love,
Till that a capable and wide revenge
Swallow them up.'

Othello, Act 3 Scene 3, lines 456–463

10

IN THE FORTY-FIFTH YEAR OF HIS AGE

From before 1604, Shakespeare had moved back north of the river, away from The Globe, and was living in the parish of St Olave. He had lodgings in Silver Street, a respectable part of the city in the area now bounded by Moorgate and Poultry. Shakespeare's landlord at this time was Christopher Mountjoy, a Frenchman engaged in the fashionable trade of making tires (head-pieces for ladies, ornamented with gold, silver and jewels). What happened next gives us a rare glimpse into Shakespeare's world and the daily life of London at this time.

In 1604 one of Mountjoy's former apprentices[†], Stephen Belott, started working for him again and the Mountjoys soon began to encourage him to marry their daughter, Mary. Shakespeare appears to have been called in to help persuade Stephen. The couple were married on 19 November 1604 in St Olave's Church, down the road from the Mountjoys'. Christopher Mountjoy clearly expected Stephen and Mary to stay and help with the business but, to his annoyance, they moved out and set up in opposition nearby. Belott believed that he had been promised a cash dowry as part of the marriage settlement and a further £200 when old Mountjoy died, but all they got as a dowry was £10 and some bits and pieces of second-hand household items. After Mrs Mountjoy died in 1606 the Belotts returned to Silver Street and became partners in the business, but there were more arguments and within a few years they left again. By 1612, anxious that old Mountjoy was going to cut them out of his will, they went to court. It was then that Stephen Belott, backed up by various friends and former servants of Mountjoy's, recalled Shakespeare's part in the affair, and that he had repeated Mountjoy's promise to give Belott money if he married Mary. Shakespeare, who had moved out years earlier, was called to give evidence but he either could not or would not remember exactly what had been said or promised. The matter fizzled out, with those called upon to arbitrate deciding that neither Mountjoy nor Belott were up to much, and Shakespeare returned to his own concerns.

Although Shakespeare lived in London for at least some part of most years from the early 1590s, it is unlikely that his wife, Anne, and his children ever joined him. Until he bought New Place, they almost certainly lived at the Shakespeare family home in Henley Street in Stratford. Shakespeare gradually increased the amount of land and property he owned in the town. On 1 May 1602 he purchased 170 acres of land from William and John Combe, scattered in small parcels around the north and east of Stratford. He paid £320 for the land – a very considerable sum which may have partly been made available by his inheritance from his father's death the year before.

Three years later Shakespeare bought a 33-year inter-est in Stratford's tithes. Tithes were originally the church's right to receive a tenth part of the agricultural produce of a parish so as to provide the local priest with a living. In Stratford these had been paid to the priests of Holy Trinity Church, but after this religious foundation was dissolved in the mid-16th century they passed to the borough† of Stratford. The borough then sold the right to collect the tithes on to private individuals who had to pay a fixed sum annually back to the borough, but could keep the profits. It was a part of this arrangement which Shakespeare bought in 1605. He paid £440 (so in three years he had at least £760 to dispose of – or was he rearranging the income available from his inheritance?). The gross income from the tithes was about £60 a year; £17 a year was repaid to the borough and £5 to another Stratford resident who retained an interest in the tithes. This left Shakespeare with about £40 a year profit. By about 1613 he would have recouped the £440 he had originally paid, so he and his descendants had another 21 years to enjoy the profits: a likely total of over £800. Already in 1602 Shakespeare was clearly planning for his own and his children's future.

In June 1607 Shakespeare's eldest daughter Susanna married Dr John Hall, who gave medical treatment to many local families. They continued to live in Stratford and their daughter, Elizabeth, was born in February 1608. In August 1607, William Shakespeare's nephew Edward, the illegitimate son of his brother Edmund, was buried in St Giles-without-Cripplegate's cemetery in London. Four months later, and at the turn of the year, Edmund – himself a player – died. Then in September 1608 William's mother, Mary, died in Stratford. The theatres were closed for much of 1608 because of plague[†], but either Shakespeare himself or someone on his or the King's Men's behalf seems to have made some use of the time by bringing a number of the plays into print.

By 1608, when he was 44 years old, William Shakespeare was a wealthy property owner in Stratford, a businessman with interests in the lucrative world of the London playhouses, and an experienced man of the theatre working with the King's Men, the company who had received King James I's own special licence. His plays were known at court and in the popular public playhouses both outdoors at The Globe and indoors at the Blackfriars. Many were published in individual editions, as were the poems *Venus and Adonis* and *The Rape of Lucrece*. Now two more printed books appeared which contained some of his most complex, profound and puzzling writing: *King Lear* in 1608 and the 154 *Sonnets* in 1609.

KING LEAR

The story of King Lear and his three daughters was well known at the beginning of the 17th century. There was even a play on the subject published in 1605, which provided Shakespeare with a good deal of his plot. Shakespeare's own *The History of King Lear* was printed in 1608 in a Quarto† edition. This may have been the text of the version performed before King James on 26 December 1606. However, a substantially changed text was published in the Folio† in 1623 and it seems likely that these changes were the result of the experience of performing the play over a number of years.

The story of King Lear belongs to a world not far removed from fairy tale. A king decides to divide his kingdom between his three daughters and asks them, before they can claim their share, to say how much they love him. The eldest – Goneril and Regan – flatter him suitably and get their reward but the third – Cordelia – refuses to join in, not because she does not love her father, but because she finds the demand abhorrent.

Lear: What can you say to win a third more opulent
Than your sisters?
Cordelia: Nothing, my lord.
Lear: How? Nothing can come of nothing. Speak again.
Cordelia: Unhappy that I am, I cannot heave
My heart into my mouth. I love your majesty
According to my bond, nor more nor less.

The History of King Lear, Scene 1, lines 79–85

Lear is furious and throws her out. In contrast, however, one of her suitors, the King of France, still wishes to marry her, because he loves her.

One of Lear's nobles, the Duke of Gloucester, has two sons, Edmund and Edgar. Edmund is illegitimate and harbours a grudge against his brother, who will inherit everything. He sets a plot in motion to make Gloucester think Edgar is planning to kill him, and so Edgar is banished. In the meantime Lear has divided his kingdom between Goneril and Regan and intends to spend his time equally with the two of them. But the women and their husbands plot to take all Lear's power away. As they turn against him, he goes mad and is driven out into the stormy countryside where he calls down curses on himself and begs nature to destroy the whole world. Edgar, who is pretending to be mad to escape his brother, meets Lear and takes him in from the storm.

But Gloucester has fallen into the clutches of Goneril and Regan, and his wicked son Edmund. They tear out Gloucester's eyes and send him, too, out into the world. Gloucester makes his way to the cliffs of Dover to kill himself but Edgar finds him and, pretending to help him jump from the cliff, in fact saves his life.

A war has been declared between France and Britain. Cordelia is with the French army but is captured by Edmund, along with Lear, who is now sane again but old and mentally fragile. Lear begs his daughter's forgiveness and they are reconciled. Edmund quarrels with Goneril and Regan (both of whom have fallen in love with him) and Goneril's husband, Albany, who is beginning to sicken of the plotting. Now Edgar arrives and challenges Edmund to a duel. They fight and Edmund is defeated. Goneril and Regan both take poison. An order goes out to save Lear and Cordelia, whom Edmund had condemned to execution, but too late – Cordelia is hanged and Lear, with his youngest daughter dead, dies of grief and despair. Albany and Edgar remain to establish good order in the kingdom:

Albany: The weight of this sad time we must obey,
Speak what we feel, not what we ought to say.
The oldest have borne most. We that are young
Shall never see so much, or live so long.

The History of King Lear, Scene 24, lines 318–321.
(In *The Tragedy of King Lear* [the Folio text] this speech is given
to Edgar: Act 5 Scene 3, lines 299–302.)

For many people, *King Lear* ranks as one of Shakespeare's greatest plays. It is at once huge in its scope, yet often intensely intimate in its feel; it would have been as at home in the great outdoor playhouse as on the candlelit indoor stage at the Blackfriars. It is a deeply serious but at the same time thrilling exploration of fundamental moral, psychological and spiritual questions, to which no summary can do justice. To engage with this play, whether as a performer, a member of the audience, or even as a reader, is to be plunged deep into the paradoxes of life. Nowhere is the gap wider between how people appear and how people are. The play swings between the poles of sanity and madness, words and silence, sight and blindness, folly and wisdom. Its main figure is a king, and so his actions – and his folly – have wide consequences for others, but he is also a father, and his relationship with his daughters is central. Lear mistakes Goneril and Regan's words: what they appear is not what they are, and it is too late that he realizes the truth. He mistakes Cordelia too: she can say nothing because she cannot lie and she loves her father as much as she can, no more, no less. The nature of truth, the difficulty of telling the truth, and the painfulness of the truth's consequences, run through the play alongside an exploration of what it means for one person truly to love another. Serious character flaws – vanity, lack of good judgement – cause havoc, but in the character of Edmund there is also calculating evil at work for which there is little more motivation than there was for Iago in *Othello*.

In *King Lear* Shakespeare draws together many of the oppositions he has explored before. The intense charge of the play in performance comes not least from an almost fairy-tale simplicity in the storytelling which can touch us deeply. An Ancient Greek definition, of which Shakespeare would have been well aware, speaks of tragedy† as awaking terror and pity as we watch the fall of a great hero, but also offering us change and redemption at the end. As Albany (or Edgar) speak the last hopeful lines, the cost of the redemption cannot be forgotten.

SONNETS AND A LOVER'S COMPLAINT

In 1598, Francis Meres, in his book *Palladis Tamia, Wit's Treasury* remarked that

'the sweet witty soul of Ovid lives in mellifluous and honey-tongued *Shakespeare*, witness his *Venus and Adonis*, his *Lucrece*, his sugared Sonnets among his private friends...'

Meres goes on to praise Shakespeare for his plays as well, but the reference to 'sugared Sonnets' has raised a number of questions. The sonnet – a 14-line rhymed verse form – was very popular throughout the 1590s. Shakespeare himself mocks the desire of anyone who was in love to compose a few, in *Love's Labour's Lost*, while having the lovers speak in sonnet-form at one point in *Romeo and Juliet*. A couple of sonnets by Shakespeare were printed in 1599 but it was not until 1609 that a sequence of 154 sonnets was published under his name. Were these composed when sonnet sequences were in fashion ten years earlier? Did Meres know the collection when he referred to sonnets known among Shakespeare's 'private friends'?

If so, why did Shakespeare not publish them when they might have made him some money and raised his prestige? The other possibility is that sonnets written in a less ordered fashion at that time were reworked into a sequence immediately before 1609. The earlier poems were written when the playhouses were closed during the plague. Did Shakespeare make use of another enforced lay-off in 1608 to rework, and maybe add to, a collection of earlier poems?

This is only one of the many puzzles of the *Sonnets*. The sequence appears to tell the story of a triangular relationship between a poet, a young man and a woman (the 'woman coloured ill', sometimes referred to as 'the dark lady'). Scholars and critics have enjoyed trying to find the identities of these people – it being assumed that Shakespeare himself was the poet. They have also looked for incidents in and around Shakespeare's life which might have prompted the poems. It is safe to say that no one has come up with a completely persuasive argument – which encourages more and more speculation.

One thing that is clear is that the sequence of 154 sonnets is highly unconventional – at times almost seeming to mock the earlier poets' practice of using the sequence to praise a woman's beauty. Many are addressed to a man with whom the poet himself seems to be in love; many of those addressed to a woman are hardly flattering, although the poet claims to praise and love her:

> 'My mistress' eyes are nothing like the sun;
> Coral is far more red than her lips' red.
> If snow be white, why then her breasts are dun;
> If hairs be wires, black wires grow on her head...
>> And yet, by heaven, I think my love as rare
>> As any she belied with false compare.'
>
> *Sonnet 130*, lines 1–4, 13–14

Rather than look specifically for events in Shakespeare's own biography to which these poems might refer, we could remind ourselves when they were drawn into a sequence and printed, even if some at least had been written years earlier. The years before 1608, we have argued, were a time when Shakespeare appeared to be at his most cynical about

SHAKE-SPEARES

SONNETS.

Neuer before Imprinted.

_____

AT LONDON
By *G. Eld* for *T. T.* and are
to be solde by *Iohn Wright*, dwelling
at Christ Church gate.
1 6 0 9.

TO. THE.ONLIE.BEGETTER.OF.
THESE . INSVING . SONNETS.
M^r. W. H. ALL.HAPPINESSE.
AND.THAT.ETERNITIE.
PROMISED.

BY.

OVR.EVER-LIVING.POET.

WISHETH.

THE . WELL-WISHING.
ADVENTVRER . IN.
SETTING.
FORTH.

T. T.

The Title and Dedication pages from the 1609 edition of Shakespeare's *Sonnets*. Now at The Shakespeare Birthplace Trust, Stratford-upon-Avon.

155

love and human relationships. This is the time of the sexual bitterness of *Troilus and Cressida*, the emptiness of *Othello* and the tragic depths of *King Lear*. A play he wrote at about the same time – *Pericles, Prince of Tyre* – has significant scenes in a brothel†, as does *Measure for Measure* a year or two earlier. Seen from this perspective, the intense emotional pain of the *Sonnets* begins to fit into Shakespeare's dramatic concerns. This has led some scholars to see the sequence not as autobiographical but as a fictional exploration of despair and loss.

Certainly this also helps make some sense of the other poem attached to the sequence in the printed edition of 1609. *A Lover's Complaint* is a 329-line poem in seven-line verses. In this it is very like the long earlier poem *The Rape of Lucrece*, also in seven-line verses and couched as a great lament for lost innocence. Many scholars now believe that *A Lover's Complaint* is intended to complete the sequence and to express, as did the lament of Lucrece, the outcome of the events expressed in the sonnets, from the woman's point of view:

> 'When he most burned in heart-wished luxury,
> He preached pure maid and praised cold chastity…
> O that sad breath his spongy lungs bestowed,
> O all that borrowed motion seeming owed
> Would yet again betray the fore-betrayed,
> And new pervert a reconcilèd maid.'
>
> *A Lover's Complaint*, lines 314–315, 326–329

FAIRY TALES

Although the style and subject matter of Shakespeare's plays change through his career, they do so only gradually and with a good deal of overlap. Plays on subjects drawn from Ancient Greece and Rome span his whole career: from *Titus Andronicus* at the beginning, through *Julius Caesar* and the bitter *Troilus and Cressida*, and on to *Antony and Cleopatra* and *Coriolanus*. The victorious Mark Antony of *Julius Caesar* has become, in the later play, a man infatuated with the beautiful Queen of Egypt and torn between her and the conflicting claims of Roman duty. *Coriolanus* picks up the conflict between public duty and private desire, although from a very different angle, austere where *Antony and Cleopatra* is full of sensual imagery, and Coriolanus's arrogant egotism is in stark contrast to Antony's wavering and uncertain path towards death.

From about 1606 onwards, however, Shakespeare began to explore a new way of writing plays, one that draws increasingly on magic for its effects and delicately overlaps tragedy and comedy. These plays have some of the qualities of the best fairy tales in which we can face our deeper anxieties about loss, or the changes of growing up and getting older, and in which good triumphs over evil. They are sometimes referred to as 'romances'.

In *All's Well That Ends Well*, probably written about 1605, the King of France is cured of a chronic illness by a young woman, Helen. The age-old theme known as 'the bed-trick', in which a woman avoids sleeping with a man she does not love by using a willing substitute, is turned on its head when Helen substitutes herself to Bertram, whom she loves, for another woman he is trying to seduce, thus shaming him into marrying her. *Pericles, Prince of Tyre*, a very popular play at the time, was first printed in a Quarto in 1609 but omitted from the Folio, probably because it was known to be have been jointly written by George Wilkins. It is a romantic tale which takes its hero, Pericles, through as many adventures as any Hollywood epic before he is healed of his suffering by his daughter, Marina, whom he had thought to be dead.

The relationship between fathers and daughters – so painfully examined in *King Lear* – is at the heart of *The Winter's Tale*, a story based on one by Robert Greene, Shakespeare's old enemy of 1592. Jealous King Leontes wrongly accuses his wife, Hermione, of adultery, imprisons her and arranges for their new-born daughter to be left to die on a distant sea-shore. Hermione pretends to be dead but actually hides away for many years. In the meantime the child, who has been saved by shepherds and named Perdita, grows up and falls in love with Florizel, the son of the man whom Leontes had accused of the affair with Hermione. Perdita and Florizel return to Leontes and seeing her, his stubborn heart melts. They go to the place where Leontes has been told there is a statue of his dead wife. He sees the statue and marvels at its life-likeness. He is told that it is a special statue and can move. But he has been tricked: this is the real Hermione and in a moment of transformation he finds his wife, his daughter and himself. The play ends with Leontes asking their forgiveness and blessing.

Cymbeline, written in 1610 or 1611, takes the style further still. It is a play of intertwined tragedy and comedy, set in Ancient Britain. The heroine Imogen dresses as a boy to seek her lover, who has landed with an invading army, and to avoid the loutish Cloten, son of her wicked stepmother. Cloten pursues her and is killed. Imogen, also thought to be dead, is laid beside him and wakes to find a headless corpse. The wicked queen and stepmother dies, Imogen and her lover are united, and peace is restored.

THE TEMPEST

The Tempest, whose first recorded performance was on 1 November 1611, is based on three sources: accounts of a shipwreck published in 1610, an essay on cannibals by the French thinker, Michel de Montaigne, published in a famous English translation in 1603, and stories from Ovid's *Metamorphoses*. It is a play full of allusions to magic and to the new discoveries of the Americas – new worlds in collision with the old.

Many years before the play begins, Prospero, a magician and former Duke of Milan, had been overthrown by his brother Antonio, and cast adrift in a boat with his daughter, Miranda. The island on which they land is deserted but for Caliban and his mother Sycorax, a witch. Prospero imprisons Sycorax in a tree, where she dies, and takes Caliban as his servant. Prospero then releases Ariel, another spirit, from the prison-tree where he had been imprisoned by Sycorax, and Ariel also becomes his servant. They all live on the island as Miranda grows up.

Prospero's brother, Antonio, is on a ship with other nobles, including Alonso, the King of Naples, Alonso's

159

son Ferdinand, and various servants. Using his magic, and seeking revenge, Prospero makes Ariel blow up a storm and they are all shipwrecked on Prospero's island. Ferdinand meets Miranda and they fall in love, but Prospero tests him by various ordeals. The nobles are enchanted and sleep, but two servants, Stephano and Trinculo, meet Caliban, who offers to be their servant. The three get drunk and Caliban offers to make Stephano and Trinculo lords of the island, deposing Prospero and taking Miranda for themselves. Their plans fail, Miranda marries Ferdinand, Prospero abandons revenge and seeks to be reconciled with Antonio (who says nothing), Caliban is given back his island, and Ariel is set free. But the plot has been responsible for a further darkening of the mood – once more, there is no simple happy ending.

Although we have no reason to think that Shakespeare intended this to be his final play – we know he wrote or had a hand in at least three more – nevertheless *The Tempest* does bring together many different ideas and elements from all his previous work. Many of these are expressed through the telling opposition of dark or angry magic and light or peaceable magic.

Sycorax is a practitioner of angry magic, and at times Prospero seems to share in these arts. He is angry with his brother, and shows anger towards Ferdinand, Ariel and Caliban. But Prospero also understands the power of peaceable magic, a curative force, creating order. Ariel is the agent of this magic, and even though he whips up the tempest which brings about the ship-wreck, the storm is part of the process of cure, the means of establishing order (Prospero explicitly states that all the crew and passengers are unharmed).

160

Magic is expressed in ritual: Prospero's magic staff helps conjure up the storm, and it is what he breaks when he says farewell to magic at the end. Shakespeare also ritualizes magic through the use of a masque at the wedding banquet – a clear reference to court entertainment but also the opportunity to bring the gods on stage in the person of Jupiter, and so add to the theatrical spectacle.

The island is a place where appearances and reality can be confused: nothing is what it seems, but at the same time – as in all the best fairy tales – the gap between what appears to be the case and what is true is closed. Towards the end is one of the few stage directions that Shakespeare included in his plays:

> '[The nobles] *all enter the circle which Prospero had made, and there stand charmed; which Prospero observing, speaks...*'

And Prospero speaks words of forgiveness – not sentimentally, but with a tough awareness of the pain their actions had caused him: he is still 'the wrongèd Duke of Milan'.

The gap between appearance and reality also has a part to play in the attitude to Caliban – the original owner of the island. Although clearly meant to represent our lower, animal nature, Shakespeare nevertheless treats Caliban with a good deal of sympathy: he may be smelly, he may lust after Miranda, he may be out for Prospero's blood, but he too has had his kingdom taken away, just as Prospero himself had lost Milan. Caliban is even allowed insight into the true nature of the isle:

'The isle is full of noises,
Sounds, and sweet airs, that give delight and hurt not.'

The Tempest, Act 3 Scene 2, lines 138–139

As Prospero returns to Milan, Caliban gets his island back, while Ariel is released into the air. Although they seem opposites, there are some telling resemblances between Prospero the usurped magician, Caliban the enslaved dreamer, and his mother, the witch Sycorax. The *Metamorphoses* of Ovid are a key text for Shakespeare, as we have seen. He would have read them at school, and they provided him not only with sources for some of his plays but also with the key ideas of transformation and resemblance which run through so much of his work. In Book 7, Ovid tells the story of the witch Medea. Shakespeare uses the description of her powerful witchcraft not only to describe some of the powers of Sycorax, but also at the end of the play when Prospero uses his magic to create the charmed circle in which the nobles will be trapped and then releases them, forgiven. After an invocation of the spirit world which owes so much to Ovid, and which shows how Prospero's 'rough magic' connects with that of witchcraft, the magician turns his back on such things, calls down 'heavenly music' and vows to

'break my staff,
Bury it certain fathoms in the earth,
And deeper than did ever plummet sound
I'll drown my book.'

The Tempest, Act 5 Scene 1, lines 54–56

The gap between appearance and reality is often a source of suspicion in Shakespeare – and there is much suspicion in *The Tempest*, as well as Caliban's naive misreading of the drunken servants. But it is also the stuff of magic and is a key idea in the *Metamorphoses* of Ovid. For Ovid the gap can be closed by love, and there is no doubt that Shakespeare invites us to consider the same possibility. Love had closed the gap between people in *King Lear*, though not before the tragedy had overwhelmed fathers and children. It brings together Pericles and Marina. Leontes, touching the 'statue' of his wife, and finding her and his daughter again, says,

> 'O, she's warm!
> If this be magic, let it be an art
> Lawful as eating.'
>
> *The Winter's Tale*, Act 5 Scene 3, lines 109–111

But it is, more simply and with more humanity, the magic of love that has waited for the right moment to bring forgiveness and reconciliation. So too, in *The Tempest*, Prospero leaves magic behind and embraces the same love which has waited for the right moment to be reconciled:

> 'Now my charms are all o'erthrown
> And what strength I have's mine own,
> Which is most faint.
>
> *The Tempest*, Epilogue, lines 1–2

11
WILL AND DEATH

We know that in April and May 1611 the King's Men performed *Macbeth*, *Cymbeline* and *The Winter's Tale* at The Globe playhouse. On 11 September in Stratford a list of possible contributors of money towards the cost of the upkeep of the local roads was drawn up. Someone added Shakespeare's name in the margin, possibly because he was not actually living in Stratford at the time (though his wife was presumably resident in New Place). We don't know whether Shakespeare ever made the hoped-for contribution: only one name has the sum of 2 shillings and 6 pence placed against it. The names on the Stratford list are in order of seniority within the town. It is significant that Shakespeare's has been added just below those of the bailiff[†], alderman[†] and steward (the town's official legal representative) and above the 'gentlemen' – including his own son-in-law Dr John Hall. Shakespeare was high up in Stratford's pecking order, even if he was frequently away in London.

He may however have been in Stratford on 3 February 1612 when his younger brother Gilbert was buried at Holy Trinity Church. Gilbert seems to have continued the Stratford end of the family business and to have been unmarried when he died. We know that Shakespeare was back in London on 11 May when he gave evidence in the Mountjoy case, discussed in the last chapter. At this hearing he was referred to as 'from Stratford' – so presumably he had no fixed London address to offer to the court. As he did not attend the second hearing on 19 June, he may have returned to Stratford – or the fact that he seemed to remember little of the incident under discussion may have rendered his presence unnecessary. It is unlikely he was in Stratford in February 1613 when his last surviving brother, Richard, died. The King's Men were up to their eyes in preparations for the wedding of King James's daughter Elizabeth to Count Frederick V, Elector Palatine of the Rhine, which took place on 14 February that year.

THE TWO NOBLE KINSMEN

James's eldest son, Henry, had died in November 1612 after a painful illness. He had been the apple of his father's eye, and was looked on as every inch a king in the great traditions of honour and chivalry. The grief when he died was immense and touched every aspect of society. The wedding of his sister Elizabeth, just a few months later, meant that grief had to be set aside. We know that during the celebrations the royal family saw *Much Ado About Nothing*, *Cardenio* (a play by Shakespeare and his colleague, John Fletcher, who was beginning to replace him as resident playwright for the King's Men; the play is now lost), *The Winter's Tale*, *The Tempest* and *Philaster* (by Fletcher and Francis Beaumont). All of these plays bring together pain and sadness, death and joy, funerals and weddings. Shakespeare (again almost certainly with John Fletcher, and probably Francis Beaumont, too) may have offered a new play (though it is possible it was written a few months later) which similarly swung between the two poles of celebration and lament: *The Two Noble Kinsmen*.

The play casts doubt on the sentimental tradition that with *The Tempest* Shakespeare was somehow 'bidding farewell to the stage'. It is a wonderful, complex and deeply moving exploration of human life and our painfully difficult (and sometimes disturbingly funny) attempts to make sense of it. The search for order never ends, but it is doomed to failure.

The Two Noble Kinsmen is based on a story by the medieval English poet Geoffrey Chaucer. Shakespeare never tries to hide this. In fact he seems to want us to see that he and Chaucer have the same perspective on the tragi-comedy† that is human life.

A month after the death of his brother Gilbert and the marriage of Princess Elizabeth, Shakespeare bought a house in the Blackfriars, close to the King's Men's indoor playhouse and near, too, to the river where he could be ferried across to The Globe. Shakespeare paid £140 for the property, £80 cash deposit with a six-month period to raise the other £60. The present-day Ireland's Yard, between Ludgate Circus and Queen Victoria Street, east of Blackfriars railway station, is just south of the location of Shakespeare's property. In the negotiations for the purchase of the property, Shakespeare is again described as from Stratford, and three trustees, including the landlord of the Mermaid Tavern, William Johnson, and the player John Heminges, acted for him. We do not know that Shakespeare ever lived in this house, or even if he intended to.

ALL IS TRUE

During the spring of 1613 Shakespeare was working on another new play, based on the divorce of Catherine of Aragon from King Henry VIII. It was called *All is True*. Although unfortunately rarely performed today, the play explores many of the most distinctive Shakespearean moments we have seen recurring throughout his writing career, which by now had extended over some 30 years. Henry is shown as a great manipulator – a man who knows that the theatrical display of power is the best way to keep power. The simplicity of the tragic Queen Catherine – seen sewing and mending, and speaking simply but eloquently when put on trial, in contrast to the pomp and show of Henry and his courtiers – speaks more loudly than all Henry's inflated language and presence. Cardinal Wolsey, too, as he falls from power, shifts his language to the simple and direct:

> 'I have ventured
> Like little wanton boys that swim on bladders,
> This many summers in a sea of glory,
> But far beyond my depth...'
>
> *All is True*, Act 3 Scene 2, lines 359-362

There is no sense here that Shakespeare is losing his grip as he gets older. The plotting, the language and the dramatic tension are maintained throughout the play, which ends with a direct compliment to James as the worthy successor to Queen Elizabeth, who herself makes an 'appearance' as a baby at the play's end:

> 'In her days every man shall eat in safety
> Under his own vine what he plants, and sing
> The merry songs of peace to all his neighbours...
> Nor shall this peace sleep with her, but, as when
> The bird of wonder dies – the maiden phoenix -
> Her ashes create another heir
> As great in admiration as herself...

Who from the sacred ashes of her honour
Shall star-like rise as great in fame as she was,
And so stand fixed.
Wherever the bright sun of heaven shall shine,
His honour and the greatness of his name
Shall be, and make new nations... Our children's children
Shall see this, and bless heaven.'

All is True, Act 5 Scene 4, lines 32–35, 39–42, 45–47, 50–52, 53–54

THE BURNING OF THE GLOBE

We know that *All is True* was being performed at The Globe on 29 June 1613. A merchant by the name of Henry Bluett saw it and a few days later wrote a letter about what he had seen:

'On Tuesday last there was acted at the Globe a new play called *All is True*, which had been acted not passing two or three times before. There came many people to see it insomuch that the house was very full, and as the play was almost ended the house was fired with shooting off a chamber which was stopped with tow which was blown up into the thatch of the house and so burned down to the ground. But the people escaped all without hurt except one man who was scalded with the fire by adventuring in to save a child which otherwise had been burnt.'

It is said that nature abhors a vacuum, and certainly entrepreneurs abhor a gap in the market. Soon after The Globe burnt down, Henslowe and Alleyn, whose Fortune playhouse had been the Bankside theatre's main competitor, moved back south of the Thames. They built a new playhouse at the Beargardens (on the east side of the street still called Bear Garden, just west of the modern Southwark Bridge). The Hope was a dual-purpose building with a removable stage to enable the standing area to be used for animal-baiting.

The stench from the animals, which must have lingered when plays were performed, would have been appalling, even for those very different times. Ben Jonson wrote a play, *Bartholomew Fair*, for the Hope playhouse in 1614 in which characters gamble, cheat, eat greasy pork and vomit prodigiously; the play – a huge, sprawling exploration of London low-life – probably sums up the qualities of this end of the popular theatre market.

The Globe was almost certainly very different. The rebuilt Globe cost the sharers† £1,400, and when it re-opened for business it held up to 3000 people. The roof was tiled this time, rather than thatched, but the main dimensions of the stage seem to have stayed the same. It is possible that Shakespeare left the King's Men at this time and retired to Stratford for good. There is no record of any shares in the playhouse in Shakespeare's will a couple of years later, although given his capacity for taking the long-term view which we saw in the matter of the Stratford tithes, it seems on the face of it strange that he did not hang on to a share as an investment.

Whatever his links with the new Globe, it seems certain that Shakespeare was back in Stratford by September 1614, when he got involved in a scheme by another Stratford man, William Combe, to enclose land on the Welcombe fields to the north of the town. Enclosure was an important strategy for the new breed of farming gentry†. The old system of subsistence farming, in which people grew just enough to feed their own family, had parcelled out land between many farmers over a wide area. Enclosure involved an agreement by the larger land-owners to bring their land together into blocks which were then fenced and farmed as a unit. For the poorer farmers and labourers this was a threat to their survival. The traditional access to the left-overs from harvesting was likely to disappear, removing a source of food for the winter. In addition, enclosure was often in the interest of providing more pasture for sheep, employing far fewer people than traditional crops such as corn and barley, and so threatening widespread unemployment. Enclosure may also have been contributing to famine as poor harvests – most recently in 1607 and 1608 – were made worse by a reduction in the amount of land actually under crops.

In 1614 Shakespeare was the chief land-owner in these fields. He seems to have been courted both by the town authorities, who were opposed to the enclosure which Combe was proposing, and by Combe himself. Interestingly he seems to have been struck down by an attack of indecision, although the evidence does point to him siding with Combe, which made the council push harder to get him to change his mind.

During the first months of 1615 there was some violence against Combe, who had been digging ditches to get the enclosure under way, but in April the town authorities were able to get a court order preventing him from proceeding. Combe did not give up, but Shakespeare's involvement was soon to be ended by his death.

In February 1616 his youngest daughter, Judith, then 31 years old, married Thomas Quiney. The Shakespeare and Quiney families were frequently intertwined in Stratford life. We have seen how

Richard Quiney had sought a loan from Shakespeare to help with his expenses when visiting London on Corporation[†] business, and the playwright had agreed to assist. Thomas Quiney, on the other hand, was less lucky. A month after he married Judith (they married without a proper church licence, which immediately put them in trouble with the authorities), Thomas was called before Stratford's bawdy-court (a local church court overseen by the vicar). He was found guilty of getting another woman, Margaret Wheeler, pregnant. She and her infant died and were buried together on 15 March. Quiney was sentenced to public humiliation and a fine of 5 shillings[†] (more than a week's wages for a labourer). One of the results of this seems to have been that, the day before Quiney was brought before the court, and presumably having told his father-in-law the truth, Shakespeare altered his will by effectively cutting Thomas out of it.

THE LAST WILL AND TESTAMENT

By the time he altered his will on 25 March, William Shakespeare appears to have been dying. The signature at the bottom of every page is weak and scratchy. As a man of property and business, with a wife and adult children to take care of, his will is straightforward and, while it gives us some insights into the situation he and his family found themselves in, it gives no real surprises.

To his eldest daughter, Susanna, and her husband, Dr John Hall, he left the houses and land he owned in Stratford, the house he had recently bought at the Blackfriars, and his other London interests (which may have included shares in one or the other of the King's

Men's playhouses, but we have no evidence for this). Their daughter Elizabeth was given his silver.

To his second daughter, Judith, he left £100 and promised a further £50 on condition that she gave up the cottage in Chapel Lane. He also agreed to give her, or any of her children still living in 1619, a further £150. If she remained married, she would get this as a 10 per cent annual interest payment. This effectively prevented Thomas Quiney getting his hands on her money and gave her some separate means of support if necessary. Judith also received 'my broad silver and gilt bowl'.

His sister Joan, the only other surviving child of John and Mary Shakespeare, was allowed to continue to live at the Henley Street house until she died, but had to pay rent of 1 shilling a year. Her sons, William, Michael and Thomas all received £5.

Other bequests included £19 for the poor of Stratford, money to provide a memorial in Stratford church, money to a number of Stratford men to buy rings in his memory, and

> 'to my Fellowes John Hemminge, Richard Burbage & Henry Cundell xxvjs viijd A peece (26 shillings 8 pence each) to buy them Ringes.'

It was a common practice at this time for people to enable their friends to remember them after their death by wearing memorial rings.

Almost at the end of the will, amongst the legal bits and pieces, he makes a last, strange but famous bequest:

> 'Item, I gyve unto my wife my second-best bed, with the furniture.'

We should not assume that this was all that William was giving to his wife, Anne, of whom we hear nothing between her marriage and this naming. She would have received the standard 'widow's portion' from her husband's goods and property. This varied from place to place and we don't know exactly what it was in Stratford, though it probably included the right to live at New Place until she died. The gift of 'the second-best bed' was most likely a token of love and affection. The best bed in a house in Shakespeare's time would have been reserved for special guests; the second-best bed was the one in which Anne and William slept.

Within a few weeks of making these alterations to the will, Shakespeare was dead. He died on 23 April 1616, in Stratford, and was buried on 25 April in Holy Trinity Church. As befitted an important and wealthy citizen of the town he was buried inside the church, near the altar at the east end, and a monument to his memory was placed on the wall near the grave. Shakespeare himself left the money to pay for the monument, which was carved by Gerard Johnson, whose workshops were near The Globe theatre in London.

BY ME WILLIAM SHAKESPEARE

Anne Shakespeare died, age 67, in 1623. She had already been preceded by William's other long-time companion, Richard Burbage, who died in 1619. The opposition, in the person of Philip Henslowe, died just before Shakespeare, in January 1616.

But many of the King's Men who had known Shakespeare long outlived him. Two in particular,

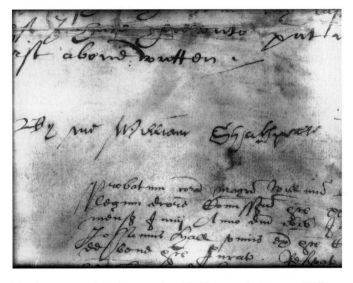

The last page of Shakespeare's will. The words 'By me, William Shakespeare', are in his own handwriting. Now in the Public Records Office, London.

John Heminges and Henry Condell, who had received with Burbage money for memorial rings, took it upon themselves, no doubt with much help from colleagues, to offer something more permanent in his name.

At the end of his will, Shakespeare wrote, as an affirmation,

'by me, William Shakespeare.'

He rarely made the same affirmation for his work after the publication of *Venus and Adonis* and *The Rape of Lucrece*. The publication of plays had always been a tricky thing. Plays were the property of the players, or their manager, and for them to be printed had for many years been to lose a precious asset: once publicly available, any company could use them. But in 1616, another playwright, Ben Jonson, had taken the bold step of collecting his stage works together and publishing them in a huge volume over 1000 pages long. This says a good deal about Jonson, who believed strongly in the right of any author to have his work recognized, published and, if possible, praised, but it also created a precedent which Heminges and Condell were prepared to follow. They too collected the plays of 'so excellent fellow as was our Shakespeare' and published them.

The so-called First Folio† of Shakespeare's plays appeared in 1623 and contains all the plays he is known to have written with the exception of *Pericles, Prince of Tyre*, written in 1608 in collaboration with George Wilkins, *Cardenio*, written in collaboration with John Fletcher and now lost, and *Love's Labour's Won*, a title which appeared on a scrap of a bookseller's list and so was presumably printed, but either no copies have survived (or been found) or it is a play now known by a different name.

The plays in the Folio often have a complex relationship to the plays that were printed earlier in separate editions. Heminges and Condell, and anyone else who helped them, would have had access to these but also to other material owned by the King's Men – possibly including Shakespeare's own copies, notes and revisions. It is a mistake, though, to think of the text of the First Folio as the only possible texts of the plays. Plays are living things. Many of Shakespeare's had remained in the repertoire of the Lord Chamberlain's Men and the King's Men for up to 30 years before the Folio was put together. They would have grown and changed with experience and circumstance during that time.

A play text is only one part of a play. It may give indications about other things – stage directions, for instance – but much else remains a matter for the actor playing before an audience. Nuances of gesture, of intonation, looks, positioning of performers on stage, costume, the use of silence, of pauses, tones of voice – all of these contribute to a play and are not contained in editions such as those of the First Folio. Above all, the plays are alive only when they are being performed; the experience of what works in front of an audience drives changes, and some of these changes seep into even the most fixed text.

It is important scholarly work to try to find a text that represents as closely as possible what Lord Strange's Men or the Lord Chamberlain's Men or the King's Men actually said, and this gives clues to the intention of the performers and the playwright, and may even offer insights into how they were performed. But the plays also have a history after the First Folio. Many of them remained in the repertoire of the King's Men until the victorious Puritan† faction in the country closed the playhouses in 1642. Quite a few returned to the stage with the re-opening of theatres after King Charles II was returned to the throne in 1660. They were cut, rewritten to meet changes in taste, 'original' texts then rediscovered (but rarely performed in unmodified forms), changed again, returned to a semblance of historical accuracy (which was, as it always is, history as seen by the present). They have been translated, criticized, read and performed countless times and across the world since 1623.

Today we are able to see how the plays were developing even during Shakespeare's own lifetime. Directors can work with the whole range of possibilities – Quartos† and Folios – to help them decide how they will engage with the plays. Sometimes this will be radical: moving the order of the scenes, or shifting lines from one place to another, or even writing some new lines in order to clarify and give a new perspective on them. There is nothing new in this approach and it is an essential part of the ongoing life of the theatre.

The First Folio is a wonderful and indispensable monument to a great playwright and man of the theatre, but like all monuments its best use is to give directions – to act as a landmark for new interactions between actors and audience. Or, to change the image, the text is a springboard for new encounters with these living plays.

❋

Year	Theatre History	William Shakespeare's Life and Family	Important Events and Personalities
c700BCE			Homer's *Iliad* probably reaches its final written form
c400BCE	Ancient Greek drama at its high point		
c200BCE	Plautus (c254-184) writing comedies		
43BCE			Ovid born (d AD17)
c4BCE	Seneca born (d AD65)		
410CE			Roman rule in Britain ends
1066			Norman conquest of Britain
1196			Stratford-upon-Avon becomes a borough
1311	First York Corpus Christi mystery plays performed		
1345	Geoffrey Chaucer born (d 1400)		
1348			Over two years the Black Death kills 25% of population of Europe
1469			Niccolo Machiavelli born (d 1527)
1490			Stratford's Clopton Bridge is built
1533			Montaigne born (d 1592)
1535			English Church separates from the authority of Rome
1538	First public playhouse built in Great Yarmouth		
1552		John Shakespeare recorded working in Henley St, Stratford	
1553			Stratford granted Charter of Incorporation
1554	John Lyly born (d 1606)		
1557		John Shakespeare marries Mary Arden	
1558	Thomas Kyd born (d 1594). George Peele born (d 1597)	Joan (d 1558) born to John and Mary	Elizabeth Tudor becomes Queen of England
1560	Robert Greene born (d 1592)		
1562		Margaret (d 1563) born to John and Mary	
1564	Christopher Marlowe born (d 1593)	William born to John and Mary. Baptised 26 April. John is Chamberlain of Stratford	20% of Stratford dies of the Plague

1566	EDWARD ALLEYN BORN (D 1626)	GILBERT (D 1612) BORN TO JOHN AND MARY	
1567	PUBLIC PLAYHOUSE THE RED LION OPENED IN LONDON BY JOHN BRAYNE. RICHARD BURBAGE BORN (D 1619)		QUEEN ELIZABETH SEES MYSTERY PLAYS DURING VISIT TO COVENTRY
1569	THE QUEEN'S MEN VISIT STRATFORD	JOAN (2) BORN TO JOHN AND MARY. JOHN IS BAILIFF OF STRATFORD	
1570		WILLIAM PROBABLY BEGINS TO ATTEND STRATFORD GRAMMAR SCHOOL	
1571		ANNE (D 1579) BORN TO JOHN AND MARY	
1572	STROLLING PLAYERS FORCED TO FIND PATRONS AFTER PASSAGE OF ACT PUNISHING ROGUES AND VAGABONDS. BEN JONSON BORN (D 1637)		
1573	INIGO JONES BORN (D 1652). EARL OF LEICESTER'S MEN PLAY IN STRATFORD		
1574	EARL OF LEICESTER'S MEN RECEIVE ROYAL LICENCE	RICHARD (D 1613) BORN TO JOHN AND MARY	
1575	ST PAUL'S BOYS GIVING PUBLIC PERFORMANCES		QUEEN ELIZABETH SEE PLAYS AND PAGEANTS DURING VISIT TO KENILWORTH
1576	JAMES BURBAGE BUILDS THE THEATRE IN LONDON. BOYS OF THE CHAPEL ROYAL PERFORM ILLEGALLY AT BLACKFRIARS		
1577	HENRY LANEMAN BUILDS THE CURTAIN THEATRE IN LONDON		RAPHAEL HOLINSHED'S CHRONICLES FIRST PUBLISHED
1579	JOHN FLETCHER BORN (D 1625)		
1580	LAST PERFORMANCE OF COVENTRY MYSTERY CYCLE	EDMUND (D 1607) BORN TO JOHN AND MARY	
1581		WILLIAM MAY BE IN LANCASHIRE	
1582		WILLIAM MARRIES ANNE HATHAWAY IN NOVEMBER	
1583	NEW COMPANY OF QUEEN'S MEN PLAYERS ESTABLISHED	SUSANNA BORN TO WILLIAM AND ANNE, BAPTISED IN MAY	WILLIAM SHAKESPEARE'S CATHOLIC COUSIN ARRESTED ON WAY TO ASSASSINATE QUEEN
1584	FRANCIS BEAUMONT BORN (D 1616)		
1585		TWINS JUDITH AND HAMNET BORN TO WILLIAM AND ANNE, BAPTISED JANUARY	
1586		WILLIAM MAY HAVE LEFT STRATFORD FOR LONDON AROUND THIS TIME	POET SIR PHILIP SIDNEY KILLED AT BATTLE OF ZUTPHEN
1587	THE ROSE THEATRE BUILT IN LONDON. CHRISTOPHER MARLOWE'S DOCTOR FAUSTUS AND TAMBURLAINE ARE WRITTEN. WILLIAM KNELL OF THE QUEEN'S MEN KILLED AT THAME		MARY QUEEN OF SCOTS IS EXECUTED

YEAR	THEATRE HISTORY	WILLIAM SHAKESPEARE'S LIFE AND FAMILY	THE WORKS OF WILLIAM SHAKESPEARE (MOST DATES ARE APPROXIMATE)	IMPORTANT EVENTS AND PERSONALITIES
1588				THE SPANISH ARMADA IS DESTROYED
1589	MARLOWE'S *JEW OF MALTA* WRITTEN		*TWO GENTLEMEN OF VERONA* WRITTEN	
1591	PEELE'S *THE OLD WIVES' TALE* WRITTEN		*THE FIRST PART OF THE CONTENTION...* *THE TRUE TRAGEDY OF RICHARD, DUKE OF YORK* WRITTEN	
1592	PLAGUE CLOSES PLAYHOUSES FROM JUNE	WILLIAM ATTACKED BY ROBERT GREENE AS 'AN UPSTART CROW'	*HENRY VI PART I* PERFORMED IN MARCH	
1593	PLAYHOUSES STILL CLOSED. MARLOWE KILLED		FIRST PERFORMANCE OF *RICHARD III* (OUTSIDE LONDON). *VENUS AND ADONIS* PRINTED. *LOVE'S LABOUR'S LOST* WRITTEN	
1594	THE QUEEN'S MEN DISBANDED	WILLIAM JOINS THE LORD CHAMBERLAIN'S MEN	*THE TAMING OF THE SHREW, TITUS ANDRONICUS* AND *THE RAPE OF LUCRECE* PRINTED. *COMEDY OF ERRORS* PERFORMED ON 28 DECEMBER.	
1595	THE SWAN THEATRE BUILT IN LONDON BY FRANCIS LANGLEY		*ROMEO AND JULIET, A MIDSUMMER NIGHT'S DREAM,* AND *RICHARD II* WRITTEN	
1596	JAMES BURBAGE LEASES BLACKFRIARS BUILDINGS	WILLIAM AND ANNE'S SON, HAMNET, DIES. JOHN SHAKESPEARE GRANTED A COAT-OF-ARMS	*KING JOHN, THE MERCHANT OF VENICE* AND *HENRY IV PART I* WRITTEN	
1597	JAMES BURBAGE DIES	WILLIAM BUYS NEW PLACE, STRATFORD	*THE MERRY WIVES OF WINDSOR* AND *HENRY IV PART II* WRITTEN	
1598	THE THEATRE DEMOLISHED JONSON'S *EVERY MAN* WRITTEN		*MUCH ADO ABOUT NOTHING* WRITTEN	GEORGE CHAPMAN'S (1559–1636) ENGLISH TRANSLATIONS OF HOMER'S *ILIAD* PUBLISHED
1599	THE (FIRST) GLOBE THEATRE BUILT		*HENRY V* AND *JULIUS CAESAR* WRITTEN	
1600	THE FORTUNE THEATRE BUILT		*AS YOU LIKE IT* WRITTEN. FIRST VERSION OF *HAMLET* WRITTEN	
1601		JOHN SHAKESPEARE DIES	*TWELFTH NIGHT* WRITTEN	
1602			*TROILUS AND CRESSIDA* WRITTEN	

1603	Plague closes London theatres from May	William's company of players receive royal authority on 19 May.		Queen Elizabeth I dies. Coronation of King James I on 25 July
1604	London theatres reopen in April		Timon of Athens written. Othello performed 1 November, Measure for Measure performed 26 December	Coronation Procession of James I, 15 March
1605	The Rose theatre probably demolished		All's Well That Ends Well	The Gunpowder Plot fails on 5 November
1606			Macbeth and Antony and Cleopatra written	
1607		William and Anne's daughter, Susanna, marries Dr John Hall. William's actor-brother Edmund dies in December	Pericles, Prince of Tyre written.	
1608	King's Men move into Blackfriars theatre	William's granddaughter, Elizabeth, born. William's mother, Mary, dies	First version of King Lear printed. Coriolanus written	
1609			Sonnets and A Lover's Complaint printed	
1611			The Winter's Tale performed. Cymbeline performed. Tempest performed	
1612				Henry, eldest son of King James I, dies
1613	The first Globe theatre burns down in June during a performance of All Is True		All Is True and Two Noble Kinsmen	
1614	The second Globe built (demolished in 1644). The Hope theatre is built			
1616	Philip Henslowe dies	William Shakespeare dies in April, possibly on the 23. William and Anne's daughter, Judith, marries Thomas Quiney		Actor-theatre owner Edward Alleyn founds Dulwich College in London. King James daughter Elizabeth marries
1619	Richard Burbage dies			
1621	The Fortune theatre burns down			
1623	Anne Shakespeare dies		The First Folio is published	

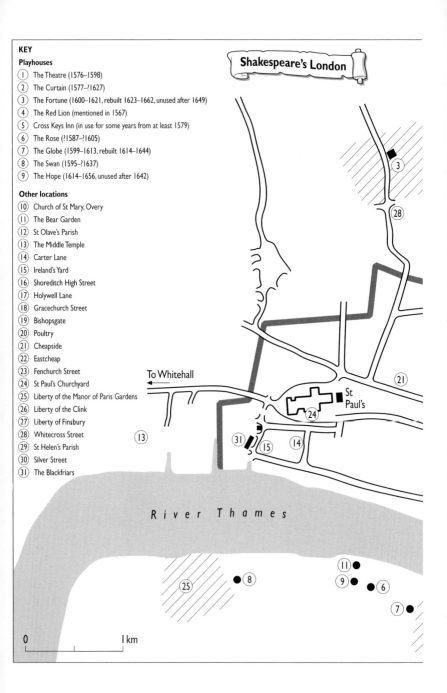

KEY

Playhouses

1. The Theatre (1576–1598)
2. The Curtain (1577–?1627)
3. The Fortune (1600–1621, rebuilt 1623–1662, unused after 1649)
4. The Red Lion (mentioned in 1567)
5. Cross Keys Inn (in use for some years from at least 1579)
6. The Rose (?1587–?1605)
7. The Globe (1599–1613, rebuilt 1614–1644)
8. The Swan (1595–?1637)
9. The Hope (1614–1656, unused after 1642)

Other locations

10. Church of St Mary, Overy
11. The Bear Garden
12. St Olave's Parish
13. The Middle Temple
14. Carter Lane
15. Ireland's Yard
16. Shoreditch High Street
17. Holywell Lane
18. Gracechurch Street
19. Bishopsgate
20. Poultry
21. Cheapside
22. Eastcheap
23. Fenchurch Street
24. St Paul's Churchyard
25. Liberty of the Manor of Paris Gardens
26. Liberty of the Clink
27. Liberty of Finsbury
28. Whitecross Street
29. St Helen's Parish
30. Silver Street
31. The Blackfriars

Shakespeare's London

To Whitehall

St Paul's

River Thames

0   1 km

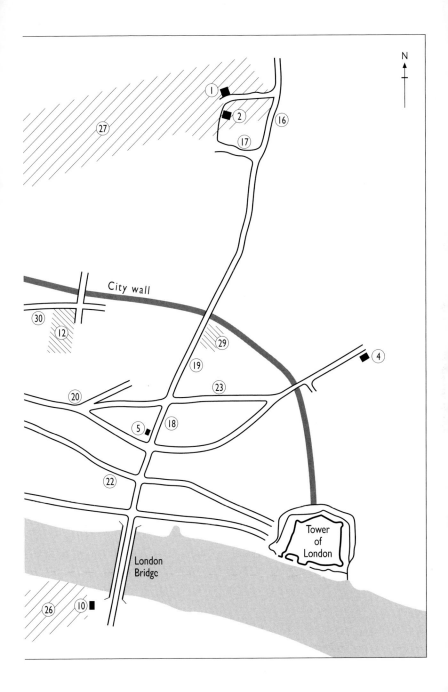

NOTES FOR FURTHER STUDY

Quotations throughout this book are from the single-volume critical edition edited by Stanley Wells and Gary Taylor: *William Shakespeare: The Complete Works* Oxford University Press, 1986. There are many other editions of individual plays and poems. The Arden, New Arden series and the New Penguin Shakespeare are clear, and have good critical introductions and notes. The Penguin Critical Studies series is more advanced, but fascinating.

The following are also recommended:

Bate, Jonathan *The Genius of Shakespeare* Macmillan/Picador, London, 1997.

Cox, John D. and Kaplan, David Scott (eds) *A New History of Early English Drama* Columbia University Press, New York, 1997.

Eagleton, Terry *William Shakespeare* Blackwell, Oxford, 1986.

Greenblatt, Stephen *Shakespearean Negotiations* Oxford University Press, 1990.

Greer, Germaine *Shakespeare*, Past Masters series, Oxford University Press, Oxford, 1986.

Gurr, Andrew *The Shakespearean Stage, 1574–1642* Cambridge University Press, Cambridge, 1980.
Playgoing in Shakespeare's London Cambridge University Press, Cambridge, 1996.

Honan, Park *Shakespeare: A Life* Clarendon Press, Oxford, 1998.

Honigmann, E. A. J. *Shakespeare: The 'Lost Years'* Manchester University Press, 1985.

Kay, Dennis *Shakespeare: His Life, Work and Era* Sidgwick and Jackson, London, 1992.

Laroque François *Shakespeare: Court, Crowd and Playhouse* Thames and Hudson, New Horizons, London, 1993.

Schoenbaum, S. *William Shakespeare: A Compact Documentary Life* Oxford University Press, Oxford, 1986.

Thomson, Peter *Shakespeare's Professional Career* Cambridge University Press, Cambridge, 1992.
Shakespeare's Theatre Routledge, London, second edition, 1992

Wells, Stanley *Shakespeare: A Dramatic Life* Sinclair-Stevenson, London, 1994.

Wilson, Richard *Will Power* Harvester Wheatsheaf, London, 1993.

ADDITIONAL RESOURCES

Royal Shakespeare Company
Waterside
Stratford-Upon-Avon
Warwickshire CV37 6BB
Tel: 01789 296655
http://www.rsc.org.uk
details of performances of plays, and background
information: also education packs.

Shakespeare Birthplace Trust
Henley Street
Stratford-Upon-Avon
Warwickshire CV37 6QW
Tel: 01789 204016
Fax: 01789 296083
http://www.shakespeare.org.uk
maintains the Shakespeare Centre Library, has details of local
history and Shakespeare properties in Stratford.

International Shakespeare Globe Centre Ltd
Bear Gardens
Bankside, Southwark
London SE1 9EB
Tel: 0171 620 0202
http://www.shakespeare-globe.org.uk
exciting recreation of the Globe Theatre, and educational
organization.

Museum of London
London Wall
London EC2Y 5HN
Tel: 0171 600 3699
Information line: 0171 600 0807
Email: info@museumoflondon.org.uk
http://www.museum-london.org.uk
information and exhibits include London in Shakespeare's time.

GLOSSARY

alderman—senior elected member of a town or city council.

apprentice—young person being trained in a trade. In Shakespeare's time, apprentices lived with their master's family for up to seven years.

bailiff—senior elected member of the borough council, the equivalent of today's mayor. Stratford had an elected bailiff from about 1290. John Shakespeare was bailiff in 1567.

bergamasque—country dance, originally associated with the town of Bergamo in Italy. The jig at the end of the Pyramus and Thisbe play in *A Midsummer Night's Dream* is a bergamasque.

borough—town whose local government is organized through the terms of a royal charter giving certain special privileges.

boy players—professional child actors, usually linked with the Chapel Royal or St Paul's Cathedral, who performed plays written especially for them.

burgess—a citizen of a borough – often with special responsibilities for the life of the town.

Catholic—a term used after the Reformation to describe those who held allegiance to the Pope. Often also: Roman Catholic.

Chamberlain—officer appointed by the town council to take care of the borough's financial affairs.

chorus—In Ancient Greek drama, a group of performers who observe, comment on and sometimes participate in the action of the play. Shakespeare uses an individual actor as Chorus in *Henry V* and *Pericles* to set the scene and comment on the events unfolding before us, rather like a storyteller.

commedia—in full: *commedia dell'arte*. Highly improvised, energetic comedy, developed in Italy in the 15th and 16th centuries, making much use of stock characters.

Corporation—town whose rules of government place responsibility on a group of elected members to act together ('as one body'). Stratford was 'incorporated' by a Charter of Incorporation in 1553 after changes arising from the Reformation led to the suppression of the Guild of the Holy Cross.

Corpus Christi—church festival established in 1311 celebrating the Body and Blood of Christ. Processions and cycles of mystery plays told the story of the world from creation to the end of time from a Christian perspective and in the language of ordinary people.

dramatic irony—key dramatic effect and situation; moments in a play when the audience is aware of something of which a character is ignorant.

farce—highly physical comedy, depending for its effects on improbabilities, embarrassments, disguises and coincidences.

folio—a book of large page size. The edition of Shakespeare's plays put together by fellow actors after his death and published in his memory in 1623 is known as the First Folio.

gentry—class of people just below the nobility who gained increasing economic, social and, eventually, political power in 16th and 17th century England.

grammar school—originally a school founded for teaching the elements of grammar (especially Latin grammar) that often replaced church or cathedral schools and made education available to a wider social group. During the 16th century many grammar schools were at the forefront of educational reform and began to teach competency in the use of English as well as Latin (and some Greek).

Guild—1 the term for a collection of masters of a specific skill, trade or craft, e.g. 'The Guild of Carpenters'. Sometimes known as 'mysteries', guilds funded plays in the Corpus Christi cycles and were also influential pressure-groups for social and economic change during the 16th century.

Guild—2 the Guild of the Holy Cross was Stratford's governing body from about 1285 until 1547. Its functions passed to the bailiff and Corporation in 1553.

guisers —a person in disguise as part of a popular entertainment – *see also* mummer.

Jacobean—just as 'Elizabethan' refers to the time of Queen Elizabeth, so 'Jacobean' refers to (King) James and his times.

Jesuit—a member of the famous Roman Catholic religious order founded by Ignatius Loyola in 1534. In the Elizabethan and Jacobean popular mind a Jesuit was likely to be a spy and a crafty schemer. For Catholics, the Jesuits were a vital political and religious link with Rome. A Jesuit who was captured was likely to be interrogated, tortured and executed.

jig—a bawdy dance which often ended performances of plays in Shakespeare's time.

Knight of the Garter—member of an order of noblemen. It is thought that *The Merry Wives of Windsor* was written as part of the entertainment at Windsor Castle in April 1597 when Queen Elizabeth I created a number of new Knights, including Sir George Carey, Lord Chamberlain and patron of the company of players of which Shakespeare was a member.

Liberties—a Liberty was an area just outside the city of London where the city authorities had little power, and so where brothels and playhouses flourished.

Lord Chamberlain—the royal official who was responsible, among many other things, for providing entertainments at court and ensuring that plays contained nothing likely to offend the ruler.

Lord of Misrule—term for the person appointed as mock-ruler of the feasting and entertainment during the Christmas period, and a symbol that authority, normal life and behaviour was being turned upside down for a time.

Master of the Revels—in Elizabethan and Jacobean times, the official within the Lord Chamberlain's office with special responsibility for court entertainment and the control of players.

mummers—popular entertainers who travelled from house to house, often in disguise. 'Mummers' plays' were often based on very ancient rites about life and death, updated with topical references and with a layer of Christianity over the basically pagan message.

Mystery cycle—the collections of plays performed at the festival of Corpus Christi. 'Mystery' derives from their connection with the guilds of craftsmen who often sponsored and presented individual plays.

oratory—the art of fine speaking to an audience – usually in political contexts.

pageant—a performance, often of a spectacular nature, on a movable stage or wagon. Many of the plays in the mystery cycles may have been performed in this way. The nearest modern equivalent is perhaps the highly decorated carnival float.

patron—in Shakespeare's time, a nobleman who supported (often financially) the work of poets, artists, musicians or playing companies, often in return for a good deal of flattery. Patrons were crucial to the playing companies: without a noble patron, no licence to perform would be issued to players.

plague—bubonic plague is a highly infectious disease transmitted by fleas that live on rats. Even today, death occurs in about three-quarters of all cases; in Shakespeare's time it was even more likely.

progress—journey by a monarch through her or his lands, visiting the houses of the nobility that ensured the ruler saw, and was seen by, the people in order to establish and reinforce the structures of royal power.

Protestant—a Christian who rejects the doctrines of the Roman Catholic Church and the authority of the Pope. *See also* Reformation.

Puritans—Protestants who felt that personal responsibility and moral purity were essential to the Christian life. In the 16th and 17th centuries **Puritanism** took hold especially among the urban merchant classes, where it also had strong political implications, challenging the ruler and the nobility.

Quarto—book of smaller page size than a Folio. In Shakespeare studies, the earliest printed copies of individual plays issued, sometimes with, sometimes without, his name or (presumably) his permission. The text in the Quartos is often different from that of the Folio of 1623.

Recusant—a Catholic sympathizer who refused to attend the church services of the Church of England, at a time when non-attendance was a crime punished by a fine.

Reformation—the religious revolution in, especially, the 16th century which rejected key Roman Catholic doctrines, and the authority of the Pope.

rhetoric—the art of fine, careful and persuasive speaking, and the rules for such speech.

sharer—a player with a formalized link with a playing company, which allowed him to receive a percentage of the profits from performances.

shilling—a coin worth one-twentieth of a pound sterling. Used in Great Britain until decimalization in 1971. In Shakespeare's time, five shillings was more than a week's wages for a labourer.

tiring house—that part of the playhouse behind the stage where players could wait for their entrances, change costume, collect extra items they might need on stage, e.g. a sword, a purse, etc. and where scenery was probably stored.

tragedy—a form of play which shows the downfall of a hero and the suffering and death which that creates, evoking in the audience a sense of pity and terror.

tragi-comedy—a form of play with elements of both tragedy and comedy, often intended to show the complexity of life.